A HEATONS HISTORY

*Stories of the people, places and events
that have shaped the area*

By Phil Page

Edited by Sharon Byrne and Melissa Marriott

Published by MOOR - The Magazine for The Four Heatons

Foreword

For many years, local historian Phil Page has been contributing an amazing
array of history features to MOOR – they've long been some of the most popular
elements of the magazine. It was a natural step therefore, to publish a book
combining a selection of the best of these features with a host of new, specially
commissioned pieces. So here it is - packed with thought-provoking photographs
and stories covering all four of The Heatons (as well as parts of Reddish).
A Heatons History is an intriguing insight into the people, places and
buildings that have helped to shape The Heatons we know today.

Both Phil and MOOR Magazine would like to thank all those local
businesses that have supported the creation of this book.

LOCATIONS

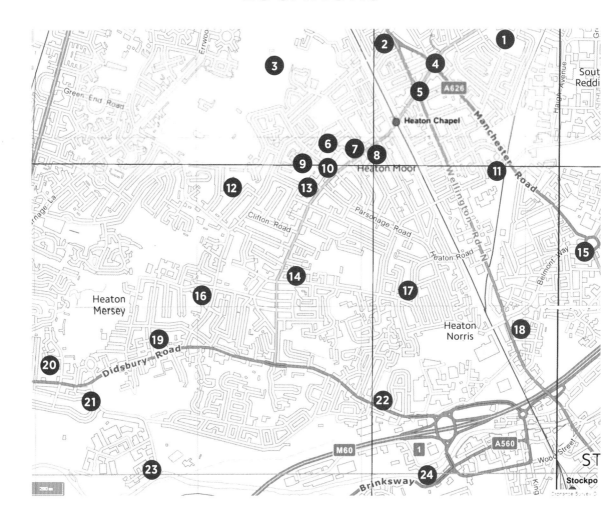

Contents

A Road to Worship

Wellington Road North

Wellington Road North! It's The Heatons' bit of the A6. One and a half miles of tarmac, speed cameras and bus lanes out of its 256 mile journey from Luton to Carlisle.

Along its length are fine Victorian and Edwardian houses, set back from the fumes and noise of the passing traffic, with a number of businesses which have gained a foothold along its route. The shops at the junction with Heaton Lane have been there since around 1900, tucked in on a small plot next to the railway bridge which straddles the once busy line from Stockport to Stalybridge. Those at the junction with Heaton Moor Road have served local shoppers well for over 90 years. In addition, there are a few established public houses, the odd petrol station and of course, the McVities Factory - which has been churning out Penguins and Jaffa Cakes as well as permeating the air with the smell of Ginger Nuts since 1918.

The road itself was constructed after the Napoleonic wars and officially opened with great ceremony in 1826. Horse-drawn trams were used from 1889 when the service started at Torkington Road in Hazel Grove, and an electrified route into Manchester was established by 1900. The trams ran successfully until just after the Second world War. They were replaced by buses which had established a regular service into Manchester by 1949. Over the last 60 years, the road has become one of the busiest in Britain, with the main 192 bus route now handling more than nine million passengers every year.

It wasn't always the main route through The Heatons, of course. During the 18th and 19th centuries, Acts of Parliament set up the Turnpike Trusts whose job it was to collect tolls from travellers to fund the maintenance of the highways. Manchester Road was the original main road from Stockport to Manchester and ran through Heaton Chapel. A tollgate was built opposite St. Thomas' Church when the road became a turnpike road in the early 1720s, but all vehicles had free access after 1873. The road is thought to be of Roman origin, part of a route which ran from Manchester and entered Stockport down Lancashire Hill. The toll booth stood proudly at the junction opposite St Thomas' Church and the infant school buildings, right up until the 1960s when it was demolished following damage in a traffic accident.

But perhaps our stretch of the A6 is a

Left: **A tram trundles down Wellington Road North, circa 1905**

Below: **The old toll booth on the corner of Manchester Road and Wellington Road North, circa 1905**

tale of two churches. At the northern end is the church of St Thomas the Apostle. It is the oldest church in Stockport and dates from 1755. The original building was used as a Chapel of Ease until its consecration in 1765. The church gave its name to the area of Heaton Chapel, becoming the first place of worship in what we now know as The Heatons. The church also lent its name to the Chapel House pub which was built just across the road in 1822. It was re-built in 1890 but now, (at time of print), following its most recent incarnation as a retail space, like so many fine pubs, it remains empty and unloved.

At the southern end, in Heaton Norris, is Christ Church, designed by Manchester architect William Hayley, and completed by 1846. Unlike St Thomas' it can no longer welcome worshippers through its doors. The church was in use up to the 1970s but around this time it was discovered that the fabric of the building was in very poor condition, including a considerable amount of dry rot - and worse was to come. In 1977 it had the misfortune to catch fire during the firemen's lengthy industrial dispute. The fire station on Daw Bank was shut and a Green Goddess army vehicle overturned on its way to the church. By the time the fire could be tackled, considerable damage had been done to the structure and the fate of the building was all but sealed. the tower, spire, and parts of the adjoining walls remain today, but the five clock bells, made by Warner in 1896, were stolen in 1977. The church however, remains one of English Heritage's Grade II listed buildings.

Above: **Shops on Wellington Road North, circa 1955**

Above Left: **Wellington Road North, circa 1902**

Left: **Christ Church and Wellington Road North, circa 1906**

Above. **Shops on the corner of Heaton Lane and Wellington Road North, circa 1905**

Left: **St Thomas' Church, 1903**

MADE
TO LAST

The Business of Building Bricks

We all love our houses, old or new, and there's a good selection of residential styles dotted around The Heatons to cater for everyone's taste. But did you know that the majority of bricks used to construct our houses and buildings before the Second World War were actually manufactured in Heaton Mersey?

Brick manufacture was always prevalent in the area, but originally only as a cottage industry, with small clay pits being dug out to provide bricks for a specific building. This was a fairly easy job across the south Heatons, as layers of boulder clay were readily accessible in a variety of locations.

The process of brick-making fitted perfectly into the agricultural calendar. When the autumn harvest was over, clay would be dug out of the fields, stacked in heaps, and left to harden over the winter months. When it was fully matured, the weathered clay would be kneaded into a plastic consistency using hands and feet (a job often undertaken by local children) and

placed into wooden moulds to harden.

In 1825 there were three brick makers based in the area of Grundy Hill, near where the Griffin Pub (on Didsbury Road) is situated today. These businesses were fairly small, but sometime around 1850 Peter Bailey developed an extensive brickworks along Harwood Road, which occupied the site of the sports ground and the former Cranford Driving Range. His site was situated on a thick bed of high-quality clay which was some twenty or thirty feet deep.

The brickworks expanded rapidly, and by the late 1800s Bailey had acquired a

Right: **A view from the brickworks towards the large houses on New Beech Rd, showing the tram tracks**

Left: **The lake created by the clay quarry, 1950s**

Below: **The brickworks and firing kiln, 1930s**

circular Hoffman Firing Kiln which was situated roughly on the site of Crossgate Mews. The kiln allowed continuous brick production. Steam excavators were brought in, and tram tracks constructed across the site to facilitate the easy transportation of bricks. Such was the success of his business that Bailey was able to 'export' bricks out of the area and much of the Belle Vue Pleasure Gardens was constructed using bricks from the Harwood Road Site. So keen was Bailey to promote his business that, in an outrageous publicity stunt, he employed elephants to move the bricks from Heaton Mersey to the Belle Vue construction site!

As the business grew, Bailey was able to extend the range of products being manufactured on the site. By the turn of the century he was producing earthenware pipes, (for use in sewerage construction), garden pots, propagating pans, lard mugs and a full range of black and yellow earthenware goods. Besides this, his production of bricks continued almost around the clock with a regular output of over 120,000 per week.

The business finally exhausted its clay seam around the mid-1960s. The site became disused and a huge pool of water developed in the area once occupied by the deepest pit. Much to the terror of local parents, it became a haven for swimming and raft-building for the youngsters of the area, and in later years was even used by anglers hoping to spring a catch or two from down in the cloudy waters.

Conscious of health and safety, the area was reclaimed and filled in by the council in the early 1970s, with the land being used mainly to construct the aforementioned cricket pitch and driving range. Bailey's legacy lives on however, in the fine red architecture of many of The Heatons' oldest buildings.

F.S. Trueman's
Coal Depot,
1900

Coal, Coke and Chrysanthemums

The Cabins at Heaton Chapel Station

The small wooden building nestling on the corner of Tatton Road South and Heaton Moor Road, (conveniently sited for passengers alighting at Heaton Chapel Station and realising they have forgotten a special occasion or some important anniversary) hasn't always been a pretty little flower shop. The building has an interesting history - it was once part of a longer line of timber structures which was home to various enterprises before it was demolished relatively recently.

The building in question originally belonged to coal merchant F. S. Trueman. It was opened in 1858 and was the office for their depot that received coal from trains operating on the LNER, the company responsible for bringing the railway to The Heatons in 1852. The small coal depot would have supplied coal to the growing number of houses in The Heatons, as it became established as a popular residential area. Most stations had a small railway siding solely for domestic and minor industrial coal supplies - but this was not the case at Heaton Chapel Station. The station did

however, have a double set of railway lines running north and south, so coal could be unloaded without interrupting the flow of the main rail traffic.

After unloading, the coal would have been moved up the steep path from the station to a small yard next to the main road, which would have been owned by, or leased to, F. S. Trueman. Local coal merchants often also traded as builders' merchants and so the yard would probably have been divided up, in order to store goods and materials not directly related to the coal business. A small coal yard, like that operated by

Trueman's, would receive perhaps three or four wagon loads a week. In more built-up areas, there may have been up to ten wagon-loads of deliveries per day. The business most likely operated a single, horse-drawn wagon, rather than a fleet of vehicles which would be found in the larger enterprises. In the photograph the horse can be seen - waiting patiently on the road outside.

The office of F. S. Trueman was close to where the coal was stored, so potential customers did not have to negotiate the dirty and dangerous yard area. At the beginning of the 20th century, the coal office also housed a barber's shop - which no doubt would have been convenient to men strolling down Heaton Moor Road on a Saturday morning to order their coal for the week.

The type of rail traffic associated with the coal depot started to decline in the 1950s and had all but disappeared by the early 90s. Many small yards like that of F. S. Trueman, shut in the 1960s when goods traffic was concentrated into larger yards to be distributed by road. The effects of the Beeching Report (which in essence rationalised the railways, closing stations and hundreds of miles of line

in the 1960s) hastened their demise.

The white tethering stone outside the Flower Basket is a poignant reminder of the past... but these days it's a splash of colour that catches your eye, (not a speck of coal dust!) and the aroma of fresh coffee that permeates your senses, as you pass by Heaton Chapel Station. The Flower Basket, which was established in 1974, and the much newer B'spoke Coffee, are the sole survivors in that little row - all the

others (including Davies' Fruit and Veg shop and a second-hand book shop) having long since been demolished.

With planning permission approved, we will see three new units fill the space of the previously demolished buildings. Built by a local company Gannon Building Ltd to complement the existing unit, each will have its own unique quirky character. Perhaps years from now, Heatonions of the day will think that they have been there all along!

Above:
Coal depot buildings, 1974

Left **Mary's Flower Basket was always popular with commuters**

FLOWING CLEAR FROM STOCKPORT

A Walk Along The Mersey

Well, it's our river, isn't it? For all of its associations with Liverpool, and its iconic tales and songs, more than half of the River Mersey's 70-mile length sits within the boundaries of Greater Manchester.

It was back in 1983, after the Toxteth Riots, that Michael Heseltine, then Secretary of State, looked at the River Mersey and decided something had to be done. It was considered one of the most polluted rivers in Europe, and he instigated a successful 20-year regeneration programme. Today the Mersey is one of the cleanest rivers in England.

The source of the river is the confluence of the Rivers Goyt and Tame, in the centre of Stockport. From here you can walk the banks of the River Mersey until it flows into the Manchester Ship Canal at Irlam, taking in some history along the way.

Right: **The remains of Oldknow's Mill, and the weir feeding the mill race, can be seen at the start of the walk**

Below: **Simon's Bridge, circa 1905**

The river leaves the town centre, flowing under Stockport Railway Viaduct. One of the largest brick structures in Britain, and reputed to contain 11 million bricks, the viaduct was built in 1840 to carry the tracks for the Manchester & Birmingham Railway over the Mersey, and of course is still in use today.

On its journey out of Stockport, the river passes by low-rise offices and the glass and concrete symmetry of the town's bus station, squeezing between modern retaining walls and

the sides of derelict mill buildings, remnants of Stockport's industrial past, before it glides under an old bridge by The Woolpack public house and past Stockport Pyramid.

On the opposite bank to the Pyramid, there are steps down to the river. Through the foliage, on the Cheadle side of the river, you can see the Brinksway caves set in the high crops of red sandstone that is a feature of this area of Stockport. Heading west towards Heaton Mersey, the water runs clear and long strands of river weeds

The old bridge at Cheadle was once the main crossing point for traffic heading south

cling to the red brick debris of long-demolished structures and the shards of concrete which have fallen from the steep retaining walls. Finally, escaping the town centre, the river flows under the M60 and follows the route of the old Cheshire Lines railway towards the site of Heaton Mersey Station.

Architecturally, the whole area around Vale Road has changed little since the 19th century, and the cobbled street still winds steeply past the old cottages, and down to the river. Here the remnants of Samuel Oldknow's mill and the weir which fed the mill race are still visible. Samuel Oldknow was a cloth manufacturer who established a bleaching, printing and dyeing works there in 1785. It was instrumental in transforming Heaton Mersey from a rural, agricultural hamlet into a bustling Victorian village with a brickworks and upper bleach works specialising in dyeing and printing.

A mile past the site of Oldknow's mill the river passes the playing fields of Parrs Wood School and flows

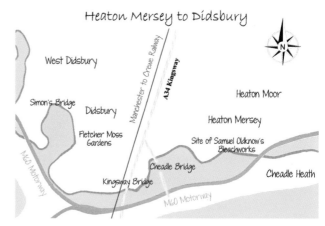

Heaton Mersey to Didsbury

under Cheadle Bridge on Manchester Road. This carved sandstone bridge, constructed in 1861, was once the sole crossing point of the Mersey, linking Didsbury to Cheadle Village. A short distance later you come to Kingsway Road Bridge. It was named after King George V, opened in 1939,

and was one of the earliest purpose-built roads for motor vehicles and trams. However, it was not extended across the river until 1959.

Strolling on towards Didsbury you reach the edges of the river's floodplain. Here Fletcher Moss Gardens are well worth a visit. This 21-acre park has

The line of poplar trees leads the way into Fletcher Moss Park

Above: **Simon's Bridge today still links Didsbury with Northenden**

Below: **'Water is Life and Heaven's Gift. Here Rivers Goyt and Tame Become Mersey. Flowing Clear From Stockport to the Sea'. This sculpture, in Stockport, marks the start of the river's 70 mile journey**

retained many of its original features, such as the rock and heather gardens, and the orchid houses situated in the Parsonage Gardens which are opposite Fletcher Moss. A nature trail winds down from the river, and you can rest at the tea rooms. The gardens are named after Alderman Fletcher Moss, who donated the park to the city of Manchester in 1919. His legacy remains today and the wildflower meadow, next to the riverbank, is a natural home to many species of plants and insects.

A little further along the banks, you reach Simon's Bridge at the end of Ford Lane. An entirely iron structure, the building of the bridge was funded in 1901 by Henry Simon, a Prussian who was born in Silesia in 1835. Despite arriving penniless in Manchester in 1860, within seven years he had established himself as a consultant engineer with offices in the city centre. In his lifetime he designed a rolling flour mill plant for McDougall Brothers and revolutionised the development of coke through the use of 'beehive ovens.' Immersing himself in the life of the city, he was a co-founder of the Hallé Concerts Society and also Withington Girls' School. Eager to help the community, he provided the monies for the bridge so that the church could access Poor's Field which provided

rent to pay for blankets and clothes.

The crossing here also has a grim history. Before the bridge, there was a ford here. Charles Stuart's army was ambushed by locals as it was retreating north to Scotland in 1745. A line of trees and mounds visible on the northern bank marks the graves of the unfortunate Scots.

A short stroll down Ford Lane will bring you to the centre of Didsbury. Should you want to, hop on the 42 bus to get back to The Heatons, or just retrace your steps. Keep an eye out for herons, otters, ducks, geese, and even a family of mink, who have made this stretch of the river their home.

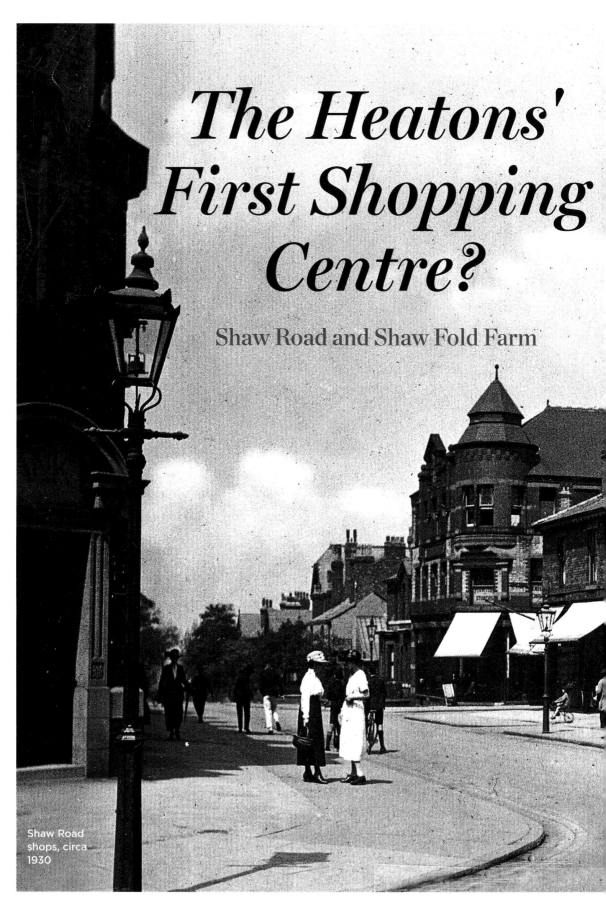

The Heatons' First Shopping Centre?

Shaw Road and Shaw Fold Farm

Shaw Road
shops, circa
1930

You could almost call it the hub of The Heatons. Shaw Road, with its bars, restaurants and regular street market is a real focus for our community. But it wasn't always like this. In days gone by it was a quiet street running down into the green open spaces which are now swallowed up by modern housing estates.

A pleasant stroll down Shaw Road in the first part of the 20th century would take you away from the bustle of Heaton Moor Road and on down to Shaw Fold Farm. The farm occupied land owned by Lord Egerton and is now covered by modern housing on Alan Road and Buckingham Road. It stretched from the end of Leegate

Above: **Hallmark Caterer's shop and van, 1927**

Below: **Shaw Road 1927 showing the petrol station to the right of the picture**

Road, bordered Heaton Moor Golf Club and West Heaton Bowling and Tennis Club to the west, and the open space of the Moor to the south. Its entrance was through a path at the bottom of Shaw Road (where St Andrews Road now exists) and there was another entrance along Alan Road - which at the time was just a muddy lane. However, as the population of The Heatons grew, so did the popularity of Shaw Road as a place where you could buy a wide variety of goods.

In the early part of the 20th century the Lancashire and Yorkshire Bank stood at the head of the road, providing a range of services demanded by the new, wealthier population and the rapidly developing commercial enterprises in the area. This bank was an offshoot of the Alliance Bank of London and Liverpool, which was a successful financial establishment, keen to expand into the provinces.

Above: **Alan Road provided a muddy entrance to Shaw Fold Farm**

Left: **Shaw Fold Farm, circa 1930**

The first branch in Manchester opened at 73 King Street on the 1st January 1864 but only lasted another seven years. When the board decided to close the branch, its enterprising manager, John Mills, decided to form a new establishment which became the Lancashire and Yorkshire Bank. The bank was highly successful and was backed by several prominent Manchester businessmen. Some of the bank's deposits were used to finance the construction of the Manchester Ship Canal which opened in 1894. Over the next few years the bank expanded its operations and a branch was opened in Heaton Moor. The Lancashire and Yorkshire Bank was eventually acquired by the Bank of Liverpool -

the Liver Bird crest can still be seen today on the wall of the building.

Over the years, Shaw Road has been home to a number of interesting and successful businesses. In the early years of the century, the corner premises housed Burgons Tea Merchants and later, Cliff and Brown, Milliners. By the 20s and 30s there was a large furniture store, (with storage facilities), on the corner of Derby Range, and a liquor shop selling Whitbreads Ales and London Stout. There was also a Tinsmith and Locksmith - advertising gas and water fitting and electric bells - and Arnolds' Cycle Shop, sitting where Heatons Tandoori is today. Hallmarks Caterers occupied the corner spot opposite the Lancashire and Yorkshire

Bank, with Meadowcrofts' Greengrocers a little further down. There was even a petrol station, selling Benzol Redline, which seemed to share its plot with Carters Ophthalmic Opticians!

In all the photographs there is the greenery of Shaw Fold Farm at the end of the road. In the late summer its fields were full of newly-mown hay, St Paul's Church providing the backdrop to a picture of rural tranquillity.

The demand for housing eventually meant that the buildings and fields were sold up for development and the farm disappeared forever. The last small portion of the Moor however, was saved and remains as a tangible reminder of the green space from which the area took its name.

Lancashire and Yorkshire Bank, circa 1905

The Poco a Poco
in its glory days,
circa 1967

GROUND CONTROL TO HEATON CHAPEL

The Rise and Fall of the Poco a Poco

Sitting in the peaceful surroundings of the Hinds Head pub, just off Manchester Road, it's hard to imagine that you are relaxing on a site that is steeped in the popular cultural history of The Heatons. The pub, which was opened in 1987, replaced the legendary Poco a Poco nightclub, finally bringing to an end decades of variety entertainment which had featured some of the biggest stars of the time along with a host of other local bands which sadly never rose to national fame.

The club had a rich and chequered history. It opened as the Empress Cinema on 6th May 1939 with a seating capacity of 1400. It was the last cinema to be built in Stockport for many years, given the forthcoming World War and the years of austerity which followed. The opening film was 'The Scarlet Pimpernel' starring Leslie Howard, Merle Oberon and Raymond Massey. However, over the next two decades, financial difficulties resulted in it merging with The Savoy in Heaton Moor and the building's days as a cinema eventually ended in 1959. Nevertheless,

the ballroom remained open as The Empress Cabaret Club with another part of the building featuring The Flamingo Coffee Jive Club.

During the early 60s, the building's main attraction was as a bingo club, but after being badly damaged by a fire in 1967, it re-opened a year later as the Poco a Poco Nightclub and Casino. Interestingly, the literal translation of 'poco a poco' is 'little by little', which was a hit for Dusty Springfield in 1966 and still popular when she visited the club in the late 1960s. There's another theory though: it was set to be named

The Ambassadeur, but the club's owner (and former Manchester City footballer) Keith Marsden, while on holiday in Spain, asked a clearly hungover Spanish waiter how he was. He replied "poco a poco", which Keith immediately adopted as the name for his club!

As its reputation across the North West grew, the club hosted a series of events featuring some of the biggest names in show business. On 7th May 1969 Frankie Howerd recorded a TV show there, and acts like Bill Hayley & The Comets, Billy Fury and Karl Denver (who is buried in Stockport Cemetery) often did week-long residences, drawing in crowds which flocked from towns and cities across the region.

Possibly its greatest claim to fame however, came on 27th April 1970, when David Bowie took to the stage just a few days before receiving his Ivor Novello award at The Talk

Of The Town in London, for 'Space Oddity' - which had been voted the best original song of 1969. The concert was organised through Stockport Schools' 6th Form Union, by pupils from Stockport Grammar School. David Bowie was second on the bill to Barclay James Harvest and it is rumoured that he slept at Stockport Railway Station after the gig, having missed the last train back to London.

The club continued to be a top cabaret venue throughout the 70s and 80s, hosting the likes of Mike Harding, Lyn Paul and The Fivepenny Piece. One of the DJs in the early 80s was an ex-pupil of mine from Peel Moat School, Michael Simmons, who worked for many years at the Merrie England Club in Blackpool. He was given his chance as a 17 year old by long term compere, Vince Miller, who, under the management of Joe Lamb

and Mike Pickard, built the reputation of the club which spread far beyond the boundaries of Stockport. With their guidance, Michael went on to become one of the top comedians in the North West and, under his stage name Joey Blower, not only had his audiences rolling in the aisles but raised thousands of pounds annually for local charities.

The Poco's days ended in in May 1987 when it was once again badly damaged by fire and, later that year, demolished. The site was acquired by Whitbread to build the Hinds Head pub. Today, the only reminder of the club's existence is in the name of the road on which the Hinds Head sits. Empress Drive stands as a nod to those distant days when crowds would flock along Manchester Road ready for an evening's entertainment at one of Stockport's most legendary venues.

Left: **The Poco a Poco was known as 'Chesters' when it closed in 1987**

Right: **Today the Hinds Head stands on the site of the former club**

Broadstone Mill

An historic past

Now providing three floors of office, meeting rooms & creative spaces to let.

a bustling present

Plus two floors of discount shopping outlet with places to eat.

Broadstone Mill, circa 1935

Living in a Material World

The Story of Broadstone Mill

It was Madonna back in 1984 whose hit Material Girl focused on 1980s consumerism and an overwhelming desire for the finer things in life. Not much of a connection with life in the early 20th century you might think. But back then The Heatons had its own material girls working long hours in the spinning rooms. Life in the material world was hard with poor pay and poor working conditions. The centre of employment and cotton spinning production for the whole area was Broadstone Mill, which stands imposingly on the southern sweep of Broadstone Road, next to the dried-up beds of the old Stockport Canal. Today it's a popular shopping outlet (with office space on the higher floors), providing a calm and relaxing

shopping experience in place of the steam and the heat and cacophony of noise from the spinning and carding machines of the early 1900s.

The Broadstone Spinning Co. Ltd., Reddish, was formed in 1903, with the intention of erecting a large double mill. Work commenced in 1906 and the two adjacent mills were quickly constructed by Stott and Sons. The building costs amounted to £480,000 by the time each mill was fully equipped (around £57million in today's money). They drew thousands of gallons of water for the condensers directly from the canal at no cost. In 1919 the mills were sold to the Broadstone Mills Limited.

When it was constructed, it was the most modern mill in Europe. It was made up of two separate units joined by a central entrance building. The complex encompassed five floors, a

basement and an ornamental water tower with a copper cupola. It covered an area of 640,000 square feet, and when completed was the largest cotton spinning mill in the world! (The previous largest, Houldsworth Mill, stands just 200 metres north of Broadstone.)

Each floor of the mill had a designated purpose. The basement contained the waste disposal area, conditioning cellar, packing room, cotton-mixing room and dust cellar. The ground floor housed the carding machines and blow room. The next four floors were spinning rooms and the tower contained the staircase, hoist and toilets. Power was provided by George and Saxon steam engines and each of the individual mills had its own boiler house. The machinery for both mills was supplied by John Hetherington & Co. Ltd. The first mill had mules with 125,000 spindles and the second mill held 140,000 spindles - giving a total

The ornamental water tower is still an imposing sight today

Clockwise from top left:
Broadstone Mill soon after opening. The Mill showing the canal. During demolition

of 265,000 spindles for the two mills.

By 1941, many of the male workers had left the industry to fight in WWII, and one of the mills was forced to close. It reopened for a short time in 1946 but by 1952 the cotton industry had started to decline, and the workforce faced an uncertain future - the mills finally closed in 1957.

In November 1958 the company sold a number of spinning mules as scrap for just over £3,000 - it was agreed

that the purchasers could leave the machines in the mill over that winter. By April 1959, a few of the machines had been broken and removed, just as the government announced a compensation package for firms agreeing to scrap spinning capacity. Sadly, as ownership of the machines had passed to the scrap merchants, it was decided that the company was not entitled to compensation of

over £60,000, despite the fact that the machinery was still on its premises. Actions in the High Court and the Court of Appeal came to nothing.

In 1960, G.E.C. purchased the mills to provide a base for the manufacture of transistors. However, following a merger with Mullards, the plans fell through and the southern mill and engine houses were demolished in 1965.

In 1967 William Baird PLC acquired the site for the production of clothing for high street retailers, once again seeing the mill providing hundreds of jobs in the textiles industry. The mill was also home to the Telemac factory shop which opened to the public in 1980.

In 1997 a private investor purchased the mill with a view to creating a mixed-use building. Today, the mill's huge red brick construction still dominates the skyline as you travel along Broadstone Road, but these days the buildings are home to Broadstone Mill Shopping Outlet, Stockport Business Incubator and rentable office space. The floors are once again alive with the echoes of the past mingling with the sounds of business and 21st century shoppers, and the ghosts of our material girls still dreaming of a lifestyle which could never be within their reach.

Below: **Female mill workers**

The eastern side of the moat facing the new Heaton Manor housing development

Below: The raised centre of Peel Moat can be accessed via a path from the south-eastern side

ROMAN SIGNAL STATION OR MEDIEVAL DEFENCE?

The Mystery of Peel Moat

There can't be many local golfers who have not at some time, paused during their round to look at Peel Moat and wonder exactly what its history holds. It's an inauspicious piece of ground, surrounded by water and populated by local wildlife. At first glance it has the appearance of a man-made lake, but it's been there for many years - several hundred, in fact.

What we can probably assume about Peel Moat is that it's some sort of earthwork. The site is a perfect square with sides facing geometrically N, S, E and W. The outer sides of the moat measure 220ft and the raised inner sides about half that distance, namely 110ft. On the eastern side of the structure is an oddly shaped entrance, but no other structures are visible. Erosion created by time and the elements have rounded off the exact precision of the original earthwork.

So what exactly is it? Over the years there have been various theories, including a hypothesis that it was created by an act of God during a thunderstorm or earthquake. More logical ideas however, have been put forward too. One theory is that it may have been a moated defensive site similar to many other medieval structures dotted around Lancashire and Cheshire. The general feeling amongst archaeologists though is that it is too small, has no recorded medieval buildings, and is not fed by a stream or river which would provide additional defensive barriers. It is also not set in a particularly defensible location given that the area around it is completely flat! There again, the name 'Peel' is an Anglo-Norman name for a small fortress or stronghold - so that adds further mystery to the story.

Another theory is that it had associations with local hunting and could have been the site of some kind of lodge or a protected area for wild animals. Wild deer and boar were hunted in the area as far back as Roman times. Another idea is that it was associated with the 'Nico Ditch' a Danish-built defensive boundary which ran five miles west of Ashton towards Old Hall Lane in Platt Fields.

The most likely explanation however, is that Peel Moat was a Roman Signal Station, similar to that preserved at Martinhoe in Devon. The construction at Peel Moat is of identical size and would have been big enough to house the 60-80 troops who might have been garrisoned there. It was probably built around AD 79, at the same time as the construction of the Castlefield Roman Fort. No Roman building materials or pottery have ever been found on the site, although remains of stone and brick foundations on the island were in evidence during the late 19th century. However, it could be that the structure was occupied only for a short time as the local tribes would have been easily subdued by the Roman legions.

If this theory is correct, it is probable that Peel Moat was annexed to the Castlefield Fort, which would have sent men and supplies and taken messages from the site. Peel Moat may have been one of a number of signal stations heading south out of the city, possibly in the direction of Chester. The structure also lies between two known Roman roads - Burnage Lane and Manchester Road - with the centre of the Moat exactly 2,500ft from each one. Local tradition has it that the site was sacked by Cromwell's troops during the Civil War and some documentary sources from the time describe the monument as having a square fortified tower.

So next time you're strolling around the area, dodging golf balls or just enjoying the smell of Ginger Nuts drifting across from McVities, take time to pause and soak up the atmosphere of the site. The sound of the steady plod of legionnaire's boots might still be hanging in the wind which whips across this exposed and open place.

Below: **An old map from around 1850 showing Peel Moat in relation to modern buildings and roads**

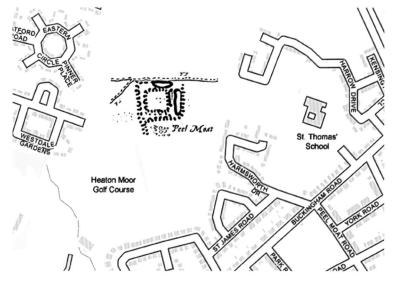

Our heart's in The Heatons!

Half a century and four generations of the same family make Joules an intrinsic part of the history of The Heatons

JOULES
Estate Agents.com

The arrival of the railway to Heaton Moor resulted in a marked increase in the building of houses

"Contentment Assured"

How Estate Agents Promoted the Dream

I think it's fair to say that most of us in England are pretty obsessed with home ownership and house prices. How many of us have actually shopped in The Heatons without stopping to check out how house prices are faring? Or when on holiday, resisted the tug of children desperate for an ice cream, as we lingered outside the local estate agents picturing our imaginary moves to Devon or Cornwall. But would we actually ever want to leave our cosy, leafy suburb?

The Heatons of course, has always been a desirable area to live. The Victorians certainly thought so when, with the arrival of the railways, they built their grand villas along Heaton Moor Road and Didsbury Road. But it was between the wars when Britain experienced a period of deflation, and house prices generally fell, that those lucky enough to avoid the effects of the recession by holding down stable, middle-income jobs, could contemplate the luxury of private home ownership.

Local builders Costello and Hammond constructed most of the distinctive 1930s housing which is a feature of Heaton Moor and Heaton Chapel. In their sales literature they focused on many of the same reasons why people buy into life in The Heatons today: outstanding schools, the quality of local shops, the availability of recreational facilities and accessibility by train all feature strongly.

With Heaton Chapel Station already established, builders were keen to see Heaton Moor develop as a key dormer suburb to which businessmen from Manchester and Stockport could escape quickly and easily after a hard day at the office. Targeting a clearly identified social group, they were quick to stress the benefits of buying a home, '... *in ideal surroundings in one of the very best residential suburbs situated between Manchester and Stockport, far away from the noise and nerve strain of both these towns, yet within easy reach of both of them.*'

However, their sales literature was more than just bare facts about the area. Without the benefit of colourful brochures and virtual tours, the sellers adopted a romantic, poetic style to paint a picture of The Heatons as a rural idyll - a place in which to settle and enjoy a particular quality of life.

T. Costello would have his buyers believe, '...*there is a 'something' about the district that is irresistible. It may be its assurance of charm, the freshness of the air, or its settled, peaceful look. Whatever it be, it suggests a new standard of home life. It confirms your sudden conviction that this is the place of your desire.*'

W. H. Hammond focused on the health benefits of the area, '...*within close proximity to the open country, free from anything suggestive of overcrowding, which gives to this attractive spot an inestimable value for those who desire bracing breezes and rural amenities ... for those who desire a healthy district where happiness and contentment are assured, we would*

STANDARD TYPE SEMI
Thornfields Estate

The General Layout is :—

　　Square Hall with neat Staircase and ample room for a Hall Stand.

　　Lounge.　　　Dining Room.

　　Kitchenette with Cupboards and back-to-back Grate Range heated from Dining Room.

　　Scullery with deep porcelain sink which is tiled round, chromium plated taps and drainer, gas wash boiler and ample shelving for storage. Pantry with concrete cold slab and ventilated. Coals—separate chamber built into the house with good accommodation.

　　Bedrooms.—Three Bedrooms.

　　Bathroom.—Built in porcelain enamelled bath and white earthenware wash basin. Chromium plated fittings. Linen cupboard contains the cylinder which keeps the bathroom constantly warm. The walls are tiled up to window sill height. W.C. in separate chamber.

　　Room for Garage, and good garden with specially constructed way-in over pavement and double opening gates.

—3—

Semi-Detached Houses

DENBY LANE, HEATON CHAPEL.

The above WELL BUILT Houses contain :—
Large Square Hall. 2 Entertaining Rooms, Kitchen with fireplace, Larder, Outside Wash-house and Coals, 3 Bedrooms, Tiled Bathroom, separate W.C., Room for garage.

PRICE £515 Chief £5
90% Mortgage Arranged.
NO LEGAL CHARGES.

T. COSTELLO,
45, Clifton Road,
HEATON MOOR.

Tel.: HEA. 1557 & 2626.

9

Above: **The Thornfield Estate was a popular development in the 1930s**

Left: **Heaton Chapel also experienced a rise in house building**

strongly recommend this particular locality for permanent residence.'

With the redevelopment of the Thornfield Estate, south of Thornfield Park, developers Sparke and Stephens continued with the theme of promoting the area as a healthy suburb, with good transport links and a host of social amenities. The houses on Curtis Road were three-bedroomed with a lounge and kitchenette which boasted a back-to-back grate range heated from the dining room. The developers were proud of their research, which had gone into designing this modern living, stating clearly that: '...*the plans have been based upon the criticism received from ladies who have visited to purchase*

**Examples of Houses in
Buckingham Road
and
Peel Moat Road
overlooking
Peel Moat Park.**

All Enquiries should be
sent to :

T. COSTELLO, 45, Clifton Road, Heaton Moor. Tel.: HEA. 1537 & 2626

Left: **Houses
were built on
Buckingham
Road in the
1930s**

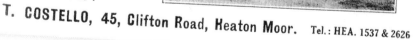

houses on Sparke and Stephens various estates.' Their brochure declared: *'When The Fog Reigns in Manchester, the Sun Shines at Heaton Mersey.'*

The vision of these builders certainly had its roots in those inter-war years, when the nation was obsessed with health and fitness and many were looking to escape the confines of heavily urbanised areas, seeking a better quality of life in more semi-rural surroundings.

Whatever their motivation they added 'a something' to the area which has contributed to the establishment of a close-knit community with its own destinct identity. In T. Costello's words of 80 years ago, ' *...a charming district where people are justly proud to live ... where no resident need spend one unpleasant or lonely hour.'*

Quotations are taken from, Green, Frank, 'Manchester and District Old and New' (London Souvenir Magazines, 1935).

FROM RURAL BACKWATER TO HIVE OF INDUSTRY

Heaton Mersey Bleachworks

Imagine if the population of the place in which you lived increased by over 160% almost overnight. The impact on your lifestyle and social well-being would be significant. It's unthinkable that such a thing could happen today, but it happened to Heaton Mersey in 1785, and the nature of the village was changed forever.

The early industrial revolution required water power to operate the machinery in many of the new factories. Rural sites were often attractive to enterprising mill owners as there was usually a plentiful supply of water to support processes such as bleaching, printing and dyeing.

These natural advantages led Samuel Oldknow to open his first factory on the banks of the Mersey, at the end of

Vale Road, in 1785. The building of these extensive works transformed Heaton Mersey from a small, rural, agricultural community to a substantial industrial village. Almost immediately, around 400 people were added to the population of the village which had previously stood at around 250.

The aim of the factory was to establish finishing processes for cotton fabrics

The large octagonal chimney, 1970s

Below left: The cottages built for the bleach workers were Park Row and Heaton Place (demolished in the 1970s)

which were spun and woven at nearby textile mills. The success of his enterprise was such that he went on to purchase a second plot of land nearer to Didsbury Road, where more cottage-based work took place. This became known as the Upper Bleachworks. By the 1880s about half the adult workforce in Heaton Mersey was employed at one of the two sites.

Bleaching was always the main focus of the firm's business. In the early days of operation, it was a painfully slow business and created much pollution when the water used in the processes was returned to the river. The newly woven cloth was boiled with lime or caustic soda and then would be pegged out in huge sheets on the top side of Heaton Mersey Bowl. There it hung for several months while the rain and sun provided a natural rinsing and bleaching

process. These areas surrounding the mill were known as white fields and it was the job of the firm's watchmen to guard them closely - day and night.

In the following years, the factories went through various periods of ownership. Samuel Oldknow was forced to sell the works after his business interests suffered financial difficulties between 1792 and 1793. Robert Parker took over the ownership and management of the businesses but died as a result of a road accident in 1815. The business was then bought by Samuel Stocks, whose interest in the works continued into the 1840s when he was made bankrupt. Mortimer Lavender Tait went on to own the business for a short time. His legacy is the block of houses he built for young apprentices, using bricks reclaimed from a demolished

chimney. They were originally known as Barracks Square but today bear the name Tait's Buildings in memory of his enterprise. They can be found just past The Crown pub on Vale Road.

Around 1860, the main site was eventually bought by two Manchester businessmen - F. Melland and E. Coward. In 1900 the firm became part of the Bleachers' Association. It not only bleached cloth but spun and wove cotton cloth. At this time the factory had 23,000 spindles and 430 looms. One of its landmarks was a 232ft high octagonal chimney which stood until it was demolished in 1995. At the time, it was Stockport's tallest surviving mill chimney. The weir, which lay just behind the chimney, is still there today, along with a few remnants of the original factory. The weir diverted water through

Above: **The Bleach Works with the railway line running across Vale Road, 1909**

Left: **Bleach workers enjoy a spot of recreation on the Bowl, 1900s**

Below: **The Upper Bleachworks from Heaton Mersey Bowl, 1920s**

a sluice and into a quarter of a mile long cut which ran through the factory, the water eventually returning to the river. In addition to the weir, many of these features are still visible if you explore the area today. The cut and the small reservoirs, which are mostly overgrown, can still be distinguished from the surrounding landscape. Under the name of Melland and Coward, the business survived until it was closed in 1992.

The Upper Bleachworks was bought by John Walton and continued trading under the firm's name of Walton, John (Heaton Mersey) Ltd., Yarn Bleachers and Sizers, until 1962. Today most of the site of the main bleachworks is covered by The Embankment industrial estate. The site of the Upper Bleachworks however, remains mostly overgrown in the area behind the houses on Vale Close and Park Row.

THE MOOR CLUB

The Heart of Heaton Moor for over a century

Snooker ● Pool ● Darts ● Big screen sporting events
Regular social evenings

THERE'S NO BETTER PLACE THAN THE MOOR CLUB

35 Heaton Moor Rd, Stockport SK4 4PB | **Tel:** 0161 432 2142

e: info@themoorclub.com | www.themoorclub.com

A Gentleman's Retreat

The Birth of The Moor Club and The Reform Club

The Conservative Club, 1907

I t's tucked away from the edge of Heaton Moor Road and sometimes swallowed up by the hustle and bustle of the Elizabethan Pub which sits next door, but in its heyday, the old Conservative Club was an oasis of calm for the men of The Heatons' Victorian households.

Of course, back then, men had more rights than women. They were believed to be better able to make rational decisions and were considered the heads of their families. As their lives ebbed and flowed between the demands of work and the responsibilities of family life, they convinced themselves that creating a gentleman's club was one

of the best ways to provide themselves with a pleasant watering hole away from the stresses of work and family.

Built in 1881, the Conservative Club came into being due to the property boom that was fuelled by the arrival of the railway to The Heatons in 1852, and the demand created by the arrival of the new middle classes who valued

Above: **Heaton Chapel Reform Club, 1904**

Left: **Then Prime Minister Harold MacMillan visits Heaton Moor Conservative Club, 1958**

such exclusive social space. The cost of the building was funded by a group of twelve local Tories who formed a limited company, 'The Heaton Moor and District Conservative Club Ltd', which was sold off in shares.

There was plenty of political debate about membership during the early years of the club. Conservatives were traditionally the recipients of inherited wealth, but the results of free-trade and booming industry allowed commercial

success to drive social status. The century's taste for change divided the Conservatives, but the members of the club seemed capable of putting these philosophical divisions aside and the club continued to grow.

Club facilities included a snooker hall, two bars, a board room and a dining suite. The club was an immediate success and by 1883 the building had been extended to include a reading room on the ground floor and

Masonic Hall on the second floor.

The club maintained strong political links well into the 20th century and received many prominent visitors from the party, notably a visit by Prime Minister Harold McMillan, in 1958.

In 2008, the club changed with tradition by dropping the word 'Conservative' from its title, merging with the nearby Liberal Reform Club, and becoming 'The Moor Club'.

The Reform Club, which sits a little

further along the road, was a later construction, appearing in 1886. It was designed by Alfred Darbyshire who also worked on the plans for Manchester Town Hall and it is possible he also had an input into the design of the Moor Club, which architecturally displays some similarities. It was used to provide housing for 'Liberal Gentlemen' and glamorous social events were held there. The building had a wide ground-floor lobby with front lounges and committee rooms. There was a large billiards room to the rear and the internal décor included marble fireplaces, moulded timber dado rails, plaster cornices and heavy wooden-panelled doors. The club was often visited by Prime Minister David Lloyd George.

Like its counterpart, the Reform Club was a private members' club, but almost 122 years since it first opened it was forced to close, after a bid to buy and refurbish the building fell through. The majority of its 100 members relocated to the Moor Club and the Reform Club building was sold on to be developed for private housing.

Happily the Moor Club continues to prosper into the 21st century, leaving behind the out-dated culture and creating an inclusive club that's open to everyone.

HMCC decorated for the coronation

Lloyd George was a regular visitor to Heaton Moor Reform Club

FYLDE LODGE, HEATON MERSEY

DEPORTMENT, ELOCUTION AND THE SWEDISH DRILL

Fylde Lodge School

Fylde Lodge School, situated on the corner of Priestnall Road and Mauldeth Road, was originally a private house, but became a school in 1893. It was run by the Misses Sales and was primarily an establishment for the daughters of local well-to-do families. The curriculum was made up of a number of essential subjects, which included singing, drawing, plain needlework and an intriguing pastime called Swedish Drill, which was apparently a series of movements the students performed in response to the teacher's vocal instructions. The exercises were performed slowly and gently (for the most part) with an emphasis on balance and complete muscle control.

Additional subjects were offered, incurring extra fees, and included solo swimming, elocution and art needlework - a type of surface embroidery popular in the later nineteenth century under the influence of the Pre-Raphaelites and the Arts and Crafts Movement. The school was highly successful and was taken over by Stockport LEA in 1921, eventually becoming the all-girls' grammar school for the local area. Standards were high: O-level results were continually above the national average, and girls were expected to adhere to strict codes of behaviour and dress. First year students had to wear velour bowler hats with the school badge on the front - anyone seen without uniform in place, or being improperly worn, (even on the bus or walking to and from school), was reported to the headmistress.

Competition amongst the school

Left: **Fylde Lodge buildings, 1930s**

Right: **The location of the school on the corner of Priestnall Road and Mauldeth Road, 1950s**

Below: **Children outside Fylde Lodge, circa 1908**

'Houses', (Peel, Warren, Tatton and Egerton), was encouraged and included sports events, a debating society, mock elections and even a choir competition.

School trips were also encouraged, regularly run by Miss Currie (domestic science) and Miss Greenhalgh (art). They often involved skiing trips to places like Brunnen and Lucerne, visiting the William Tell statue in Altdorf, and riding the cable cars and ski lifts to the tops of mountains.

In 1966 the school moved to new premises on Priestnall Road and after further educational reorganisation, became Priestnall School. The land on which the original school stood was sold for development in 1990 - some of the original buildings were incorporated into the modern structure and the apartment complex was named 'College Court'.

Priestnall still keeps a small piece of Fylde Lodge's heritage. The statue of a lion holding a shield in the school quad bears an original inscription from Fylde Lodge School.

KEEP YOUR HOME'S HISTORY ALIVE

...with contemporary period flooring

Bramley
Carpets
established 1996

139 Heaton Moor Road, Heaton Moor, Stockport. SK4 4HY

0161 432 8685 | **www.bramleycarpets.co.uk**

Carpets and rugs over solid wooden flooring were popular in the Edwardian home

A Case of Cold Feet?

Victorian and Edwardian Flooring

Look in any house in The Heatons and you'll find a variety of flooring styles, from traditional carpets through to vinyl, laminates, tiles and beautifully polished original wooden floors. Those people who own older houses take pride in preserving (or recreating) the tastes of the Victorians and Edwardians who once lived there.

Those of you who grew up in the 1950s will no doubt remember how your feet felt on the cold lino, as you hopped out of bed and hurtled down to the living room for a bit of warmth. Placing a soft covering of some sort on a hard floor has been popular for centuries. The need to create a barrier between our feet and the cold isn't new - our earliest ancestors most likely used strewn plant materials or animal skins before the the invention of weaving and creating fabrics.

In The Heatons, the newly-built houses owned by prosperous Victorians would have had rugs in the main living areas, runner carpets along passageways and up the stairs, and quarry tiles on floors that needed to withstand heavier wear and tear.

Because the area was semi-rural at this time, the smaller, less grand houses and cottages would have had floor coverings reminiscent of earlier centuries - such as compacted clay or stone or brick laid on earth. Comfort was not something many Victorians experienced in their homes - in winter the icy cold would permeate up from the ground into the living areas.

Recently, the return of stair rods has proved to be popular amongst those wishing to recreate a Victorian style in their homes. Originally used for practical purposes in those lower-middle to upper-class Victorian Heatons houses which featured wooden staircases covered by stair runner carpets, they proved to be a stylish addition with the added benefit that the runner could be pulled up or down as necessary to avoid the nose of the stair rubbing or fading the carpet in any one place. However, this practice of moving the stair runner up or down to prolong its life could promote carpet slippage – causing accidents which resulted in unsuspecting homeowners arriving at the bottom of their staircase rather sooner than intended!

Wealthier households quickly made use of large carpets for beauty and comfort on their floors. The Industrial Revolution reduced the cost of manufacturing carpets, but even so, it wasn't until the 20th century that power machinery and synthetic fabrics allowed the creation of carpet in multiple yard sizes to fit entire rooms.

One of the most popular floor coverings for Victorians was tiles. In many of the older Heatons properties they are still in place, and beautifully preserved. Initially, their high cost meant that only the very rich could afford them, and usually their use would be limited to entrances and hallways, which were of course the first areas visitors would see and therefore important for creating a real impression.

The Victorians had plenty of choice, as manufacturers started producing their tiles in all manner of shapes and sizes: triangles, diamonds, lozenges and hexagons. Wealthy families enjoyed mixing and matching different colours and shapes and they soon became the standard floor decoration for most homeowners. Laying individual tile pieces together was a laborious and expensive process that only the most skilled tilers could undertake. Once laid, a housemaid would have the unenviable task of scrubbing, waxing and buffing the tiles, to stop the natural clay absorbing dirt and grime. Those Heatonians who still have such tiles in their properties will no doubt empathise with the effort it took to maintain their beauty.

Above: **This house on Parsonage Road has the original classic Victorian hall tiles**

Right: **Stair rods were a fashionable feature of Victorian houses**

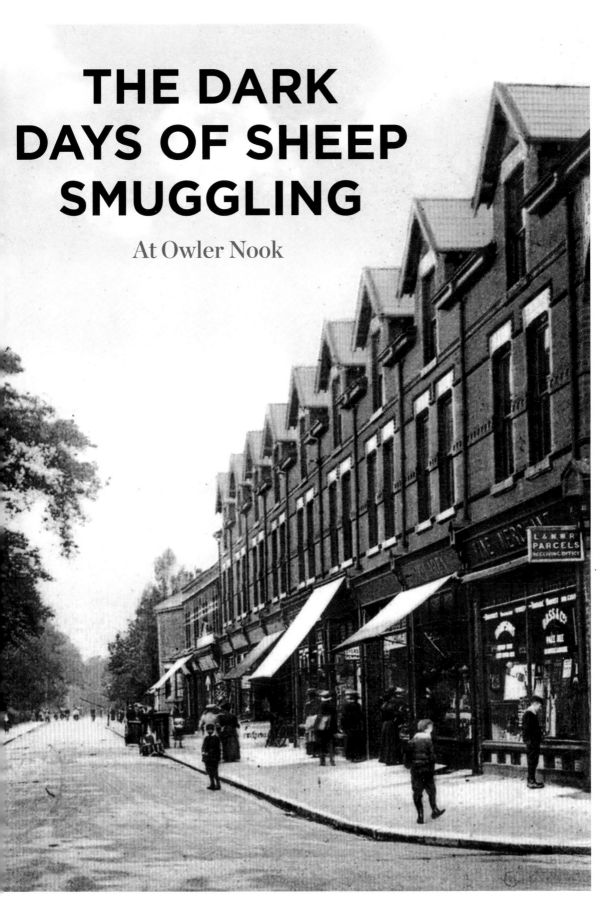

THE DARK DAYS OF SHEEP SMUGGLING

At Owler Nook

One of the things you notice most about looking at old maps is how place names have changed - or indeed disappeared altogether. The names of these places hold a linguistic fascination all of their own and there are plenty dotted around on old maps of The Heatons to get the mind thinking. Priestnall Hey, Alegar Fold, Holly Point, Meadow Bank, Lambs Fold and others are all confined to the mists of times past, but one name really intrigues me and it's a place we all know well. The busy junction of Green Lane, Heaton Moor Road and Moorside Road is known to us all as Moor Top. But over a hundred years ago it was known to all and sundry as the mysterious Owler Nook.

The name certainly gives a bit of romantic mystery to the area. 'Nook', of course, is a term still used today to describe a secret corner, or place of seclusion. 'Owler', however, is an old name for a smuggler or a dealer in contraband. It's also an archaic term for an illegal dealer in sheep, which could be relevant to the rural nature of the area at that time. Sheep smuggling was a common practice in old England and was outlawed as early as 1367. The illegal wool trade between England and France resulted in sheep being moved to ports where they, or their wool, would be loaded onto 'owling boats.' In rural areas like The Heatons, the animals would have been moved secretly under the cover of darkness (traditionally the time of the owl!).

Around 1860, little existed around Owler Nook, it sat between the well-established village of Heaton Mersey and the developing residential area around Heaton Chapel Station. Maps from the same time reveal that there was a rope-maker's premises and a few humble residential dwellings. Housing development eventually crept further south along Heaton Moor Road however, and the familiar row of shops which we know today, was constructed in 1872.

By the outbreak of the First World War Owler Nook was no longer the secluded place of the early 19th century. It had become a thriving area in its own right and more shops had appeared at the top of Moorside Road. Many of the businesses were similar to ones that exist today including a bakery and a greengrocer's. Along the narrow passage of Moor Top Place, Samuel Bates' rope business continued to thrive alongside Thomas O'Donnell's smithy.

On the opposite side to the shops stood three large buildings: Berne Cot, Dunbar and Beech House. Berne Cot was built in Colonial style by its owner who had returned to the Moor after service in the Bengal Lancers. Beech House was demolished in the 1970s to make way for a new supermarket, but the upper storeys of Berne Cot and Dunbar can still be seen above the modern shop frontages.

The buildings around Moor Top have changed little since the later days of Owler Nook. Tradespeople and shoppers mingle together much as they have done on this spot for over 100 years.

However, next time the shops are closed, and you are standing on the corner of Moorside Road after sunset, try to imagine you are back in Owler Nook on a starless, bat-black night. Your ear might just pick up the faint sound of the furtive bleating of sheep passing in the dark, destined for some foreign land.

Above: **Moor Top Shops, 1900**

Left: **Moor Top, 1906**

Right: **Berne Cot can easily be seen behind the wall and hedging**

Bowling became a popular pastime

Anyone for Tennis?

A Hundred and Fifty Years of a Sporting Institution

It's not a place you'd stumble across easily. It's tucked away like a hidden treasure just along a path which leads you away from one of The Heatons' most picturesque roads. West Heaton Bowling, Tennis and Squash Club, off Princes Road in Heaton Mersey, has been with us for a long time. In fact it's probably the oldest surviving institution in The Heatons which still plies its original trade. Imagine a time without United, City or County football teams. A time before the modern Olympics, the invention of the telephone and a time when England and Australia had yet to play each other at cricket. This club pre-dates all of these, having been formed in July 1873. Which means it has been part of Heatons life for nearly a century and a half.

The late nineteenth century saw real growth in the population of The Heatons, with a consequent demand for recreational activities for the new, wealthy families who were moving in. Typically suburban games such as golf, lawn tennis and bowling were very popular – and places to play them were needed.

Bowling and croquet were the first sports to be offered at the West Heaton club after its formation in 1873, with lawn tennis arriving in 1880 - it was a popular new activity. The modern game had only been established during the opening year of the club and the first Wimbledon Tennis Championships had only arrived three years earlier, in 1877. There was no doubt that West Heaton was at the forefront of promoting these recreational activities within the local community, with many local clubs

and teams forming, and any initial worries about the club's viability were alleviated as it went from strength to strength. Indeed, it was so successful that the original lease of the land, which ran for 17 years, was extended for a further 11 years and the freehold purchased in 1921 for a sum of £450 (around £22,000 in today's money).

The period of the First World War was a challenging time for the West Heaton club. More than twenty members enlisted in the armed forces, and throughout the war, the club did what it could to help the war effort. From Stepping Hill Hospital, and the Red Cross hospitals in Heaton Mersey, Greek Street and Hollywood, injured soldiers were invited to use the greens to help in their recuperation. Although the bowling tournaments continued throughout the war years, other activities such as the annual garden party and the whist drive were cancelled. Towards the end of the war, nearly all available members had joined the armed service. Nine members died in the fighting, and as well as their names appearing on the local War Memorial, they were remembered in a copper plate, commissioned for the purpose, which would hang in the tea room at the club.

The club has continued to move with the times and invest in new facilities: in the 1970s West Heaton built the first of its squash courts. The origins of this popular sport pre-date even the club itself: it developed from the older game of rackets, played in London's prisons in the 18th century. Around 1830, boys playing rackets at Harrow School noticed that a punctured ball, which 'squashed' on impact with the wall, made the game more challenging and physically demanding – and so the game of squash was born!

It quickly spread to other schools and by the late 19th century had increased in popularity, with various schools and clubs building squash courts.

Over the years there have been a couple of interesting 'lost and founds' at the club. The Oundle Woods were first presented as a bowling competition prize at West Heaton in 1886. They subsequently disappeared and for years afterwards there was no trace of them - until a lady in the Northamptonshire town of Oundle found them in an old box in her attic and passed them on to

the president of Oundle Bowling Club. This resulted in adverts being placed in flat green bowling magazines in an attempt to trace the former owners. As these were the days before the internet, it was quite by chance that one of the adverts was spotted by Jack Smith in Cheadle who recognised the connection with West Heaton club. And so the competition prize, first presented by William Adam to Alexander Adam, was returned to its place of origin at West Heaton. These days, the President opens the bowling season by playing an end with the 'Oundle Woods'!

In the 1970s there was an even more poignant discovery. The copper war memorial depicting the names of members who had died in the Great War had previously disappeared, but was found in a Manchester mill and returned to the club. Today it hangs in the bar, a permanent reminder of the sacrifice made by so many young men at that time.

Above: **The memorial to those members who died during WWI. The name of the 9th member, H Ashley, does not appear on the plaque**

Below: **The Heaton Mersey Ladies Bowling Club, the champions of Stockport Ladies Bowling League, 1938**

Above: **The Oundle Woods sitting proudly on the bowling green**

Left: **The inscription showing the first presentation details from 1886**

Right:
The tennis courts and clubhouse, 1954

HOSPITALS, HEROES AND THE HOME GUARD

The Heatons at War

Though possible to fill a whole book with stories from The Heatons during the first and second World Wars, I have focused on just a few elements of how those terrible conflicts impacted on the local area: the temporary Red Cross hospitals set up during WWI, the bravery and work done by The Home Guard and The Air Raid Precautions Wardens, the bomb damage to The Heatons in WWII and the story behind the only woman named on the War Memorial on Heaton Moor Road.

Back From The Front - The Heatons WWI

The shining bronze statue of a soldier in battle dress stands high on its pedestal outside St Paul's Church on Heaton Moor Road. Its bronze panels record the names of those from The Heatons who died in the greatest conflict in human history.

The statue was designed by Manchester sculptor John Cassidy, with the original estimate of the cost being between £1800 and £2000. The completed memorial was unveiled

in January 1922 and Cassidy agreed not to use the same model for any other memorial within a thirty mile radius. His work was described in the press as a statue which "suggested great ideals.... something of the infinite.... heroic endurance and sustained fortitude and triumph in the face of overwhelming odds."

Many Heatonians however, did return from the conflict, often on casualty trains which carried the injured back from the front to be looked after in the safety of their home town. The sheer number of casualties meant that existing

Left: **Heaton Moor War Memorial and St. Paul's Church**

Below: **Red Cross Hospital Treatment Ward, 1917**

Left: **Red Cross Hospital Recreation Room, 1917**

Right: **Red Cross Hospital Kitchen, 1917**

Below right: **ARP volunteers, Brownsville Road, 1941**

hospitals could not cope with so many men being returned from the front, so temporary Red Cross hospitals were set up to support the medical services. The Heatons had two such hospitals ready to receive its wounded heroes: these were situated in the Reform Club on Heaton Moor Road, and in the Methodist Church Hall on Cavendish Road. They were organised by the local committee of the Red Cross but the key player in The Heatons' organisation was an ex-teacher named Walter Brownsword.

Walter was well known in The Heatons and although he was too old to enlist, he was keen to help with the war effort. He had connections with St Paul's Church and the first Red Cross working party was set up in the church under his direction.

Each night the male volunteers would travel to Stockport station or Heaton Mersey station, to meet the trains and load the stretcher cases into waiting ambulances. When the injured were safely settled in the hospitals, the volunteers busied themselves cleaning the wards, making tea and helping the nurses. They often stayed all night,

leaving at 06.00 in the morning, getting home for just an hour's rest before getting the train to work in Manchester.

The vast majority of the work in the wards was done by the female volunteers who rolled bandages, made shirts, knitted clothes and helped to run the hospital canteens. They cleaned and washed the hospital uniforms, (which were bright blue), and wheeled the men out into the sunshine on bright days to recover in the clean, fresh air of the village.

The nursing was carried out by VADs (Voluntary Aid Detachment nurses) who ran the wards and supported doctors in administering treatment to wounds as well as implementing recuperation programmes. Walter was a great believer in the power of recreational activities to help recovery and raised money to have billiard tables and pianos installed in the wards for those men who were close to regaining their health.

There are officially 53 'Thankful Villages' in the UK - settlements in both England and Wales (none in Scotland or Ireland) from which all local members of the armed forces survived World

War I. They have no memorials to The Great War and no losses to mourn as all their men came home. It was not so in The Heatons, and Cassidy's memorial contains the names of the 126 men and one woman who lost their lives in the conflict, a symbol of how, in the majority of cities, towns and villages, all members of the community were in some way touched by the unforgettable events unfolding in those foreign fields.

The Heatons Air Raid Precautions Wardens

Like all towns which were under the threat of attack, Stockport had its full complement of Air Raid Precautions (ARP) wardens. Those volunteers who were active in Heaton Moor were stationed on Brownsville Road. ARP wardens enforced the blackout, making sure heavy curtains or shutters were present in private houses to prevent light escaping and thus making them a possible target for enemy bombers. By early 1938 some 200,000 people

had volunteered for the service and this rose to 700,000 after the Munich Agreement later that year. This was a settlement reached by Nazi Germany, Great Britain, France, and Italy allowing German annexation of the Sudetenland, in western Czechoslovakia. It was clear that Hitler was planning to occupy Czechoslovakia and war with Germany became a strong likelihood.

ARP wardens also operated air raid sirens, guided people into public air raid shelters, issued and checked the operation of gas masks, bravely evacuated areas around unexploded bombs, helped with the rescue of casualties from bomb-damaged properties, located temporary accommodation for those who had been bombed out, and reported to their local control centre about incidents which needed immediate attention. Some of the volunteers were allocated to serve in the Auxillary Fire Service which supported local firefighters during bombing raids.

Local youngsters were also involved in defence operations. Often Boy Scouts or Boys' Brigade members aged between 14 and 18 were used as runners to take messages from wardens and carry them to either the sector post or the control centre. These messengers performed an important role in providing the ARP wardens with a fuller picture of events as there was no guarantee that telephone communications would be active after a bombing raid.

The blackout had a major impact on life in The Heatons. At St Paul's Church it made evening services impossible in the winter and so these had to be held in the afternoon. Social activities were limited, but the Sunday School continued throughout the war. An air-raid shelter was made in the cellars under the choir vestry as a precaution against any sudden raids.

After the bombing of the district in December 1940, the Rector wrote in the Church magazine, *"Our losses might have been greater but for the devotion*

of the ARP, and other workers, and their prompt dealing with incendiary bombs. Some landed on the roof of the Red Cross Hospital in the parish but were successfully dealt with."

Tribute was also paid to the ladies who kept the canteen services going throughout the Blitz until ordered to close by an officer who then arranged for a group of soldiers to escort them home.

In 1941 the ARP officially changed its title to Civil Defence Service to reflect the wider range of roles it then encompassed. During the war, almost 7,000 Civil Defence workers were killed. Thankfully, there were no casualties in The Heatons.

The Home Guard

In 1908, Swiss entrepreneur Hans Renold, bought several acres of land on the border between Heaton Mersey and the Manchester suburb of Burnage. His eight-year building programme resulted in one of the largest chain manufacturing

Left: **Soldiers outside Cavendish Road Methodist Church, 1917**

Right: **Bomb damage to the Alice Briggs Hostel**

Below: **Renolds Chains' Home Guard Platoon, 1941**

plants in the country, which employed several hundred local workers. The site contained many recreational facilities including tennis courts and bowling greens, as he believed in the importance of providing increased leisure opportunities for his workers. As a security measure his company even had its own Home Guard which paraded proudly within the grounds of the factory and the wider community.

The Home Guard was originally known as the Local Defence Volunteers (LDV) and at one time were known by the rather unkind nickname of 'Look, Duck and Vanish'. However, the work done by the Home Guard was very important. Their role was to slow down the enemy even by a few hours to give the regular forces time to regroup. They defended key points of communication and factories (like Renold's) which would have been key targets for the enemy in the event of an invasion. In fact they continued to man roadblocks and guard airfields, factories and explosive stores throughout the war.

Above: **Bomb damage to houses on Didsbury Road, December 1940**

Right: **Gertrude Powicke's name inscribed on the Heaton Moor War Memorial**

Men aged 17-65 could join although, as portrayed in the popular TV comedy Dad's Army, the upper age limit was not strictly enforced. They were finally disbanded on 31 December 1945, eight months after Germany's surrender.

Gertrude Powicke

Engraved on the plinth of the War Memorial at St Paul's Church in Heaton Moor, you'll find the name Gertrude Mary Powicke. She is believed to be the only woman commemorated on any memorial in the Borough of Stockport. She was a civilian, and her date of death at the age of 32, is recorded as 20th December 1919.

Gertrude was born on the 19th December 1887 in the Hatherlow area of Romiley. She grew up in the local parsonage, where her father

Frederick was the minister of the local Congregational Church. After attending boarding school in Kent, Gertrude returned to Manchester. She was an exceptional student, starting at the Victoria University of Manchester in 1908 and graduating with a degree in Modern Languages in 1911. Following the completion of her studies, she moved on to become a teacher at the Manchester High School for Girls between the years 1911-1913. When war was declared in 1914, she was keen to go into service. She joined the war effort, learned to drive, and trained as a nurse.

In 1915 she joined the Friends Emergency and War Victims Relief Committee which had been formed by the Quakers. It undertook medical duties, including founding a maternity hospital at Chalons-

sur-Marne. Gertrude worked in France, but it is not known where.

In 1919 she travelled to Poland to treat an outbreak of Typhus. The epidemic, caused by the sudden surge of refugees returning to their farmlands after the war, was ravaging both the Polish people and the Ukrainians. Gertrude described the horrors of the refugee camps in one of her last letters home: *"I think it's one of the saddest sights I've ever seen, they have come in in hundreds, sometimes thousands and there is no wood or coal to heat the barracks... If only people in England knew how terrible it is out here, I'm sure they would be running head over heels to help."*

Gertrude travelled through many areas of war-ravaged Europe. She was nursing in the area of Lemberg when she contracted Typhus herself. She was hospitalised on her return to Warsaw but sadly died on 20th December 1919. She was buried in the Evangelical-Reformed cemetery in Warsaw. Her death was felt very strongly in England and contributions of clothing and money for the Polish relief effort were collected by the Manchester Women's Union in her name.

Her name is inscribed on the University of Manchester War Memorial and also on the family grave at Hatherlow Churchyard. It is likely that her name was added to our Heaton Moor memorial as a tibute to her because she was from Stockport and it was a new memorial.

Next time you're passing the Heaton Moor war memorial, take a little time to seek out Gertrude. She is resting peacefully on the north side of the plinth with the Joys and the Sackets.

Bomb Damage Along Didsbury Road in WWII

During the Second World War, the most significant local bomb damage from German air raids occurred on the night of 22nd December 1940, as a result of aircraft jettisoning surplus bombs after raids on Manchester which had caused a huge amount of damage across the city. More than 4,000 Manchester houses were damaged beyond repair and a further 12,000 significantly damaged during the nights of 22nd, 23rd and 24th December.

Most of the bombs dropped were high explosive devices, but the aircraft carried a smaller number of aerial mines. These were attached to parachutes to act as blast bombs and detonated at roof level rather than on impact with the ground or buildings. They were highly effective in causing widespread damage as the shock waves from the explosion were not cushioned by surrounding buildings and they had the potential to destroy whole streets of houses.

On the night of 22nd December, a returning aircraft dropped three bombs in quick succession in the Didsbury Road area. The first landed on the Alice Briggs Hostel situated on what is now the Briars Mount Housing development. The hostel, originally used by Manchester Education Committee as an educational boarding school for vulnerable girls, was completely destroyed, and the resulting blast severely damaged the line of houses opposite, on Didsbury Road.

Repair work commencing on Didsbury Road houses, early 1941

Right: **A modern Didsbury Road**

An ARP warden maintained that on the night of the raid, although history records the hostel as being empty, there were in fact, a small number of boys inside when the bomb hit. Unbelievably, the matron had locked the boys inside (the hostel's use had changed to a boys' school by this time) and then fled to the safety of the nearby Stockport shelter. The ARP warden attended the hostel after the bomb exploded and, with the aid of another warden, was able to get the children out alive. The incident was reported to the police, and the matron was arrested

but no further information seems to be available as to what happened next.

The second bomb dropped on Ryde Avenue behind the Didsbury Road houses and completely destroyed two of the houses. Amazingly the occupants escaped unscathed - a young baby was found hanging upside down and was rescued by her mother. The houses have since been re-built but can be distinguished by the slightly different colour of the bricks.

The third bomb fell on land which was then part of Heaton Norris Farm, causing no injuries or damage.

The biggest raid on The Heatons took place on 8th May 1941 when the Fairey Aviation factory at Heaton Chapel was one of the major targets. At the time it was involved in producing Hendon night bombers and would have therefore been a target of significance for the Germans.

Though The Heatons didn't suffer nearly the level of damage that some towns and cities did, the war memorials on Heaton Moor Road, outside St John's Church in Heaton Mersey, and in Houldsworth Square in Reddish, are there rightly to remind us all of the human cost of the conflicts.

Meet Me on the Corner?

Heaton Chapel Village

I t's one of The Heatons' most interesting corners. An intersection of roads surrounded by an intriguing assortment of shops and business premises. The crossroads at the junction of Manchester Road, Broadstone Road and School Lane in Heaton Chapel has been part of Heatons community life for a long time now. It's developed and changed, like many such areas do, but it still retains its character and village feel. On a good day it's alive with people eating and drinking, or shopping in a great local butcher's. It even has its own goldsmith to stamp a hallmark on the whole area!

The nearby presence of St Thomas' Church resulted in the development of the area, with many shops and businesses contributing to the emergence of Heaton Chapel village. Some of the earliest recorded businesses were Caldwell's haberdasher's, Brearley's ice cream shop and a wallpaper shop.

Manchester Road was once known as the High Street and was the principal route south as you entered the outskirts of Stockport. Wellington Road was yet to bridge the Mersey and traffic had to pass through a toll gate at the intersection of

the roads before heading south down Dodge Hill and across the Mersey at Lancashire Bridge. It also marked the route of the old Roman Road which ran from Manchester on to Buxton.

The area has an interesting history of its own. The southern corner of the junction was once the location of a school run by the Hollinpriest Charity. The organisation was prevalent in the area around the late 1700s and early 1800s. School Lane takes its name from the charity, and the school existed for a further 100 years, until the beginning of the 20th century. In its later years it was known as Travis's School after its headmaster, William Travis. William was quite a local character and presided over the school for fifty years. When he died, a memorial to commemorate his life was commissioned and erected in St. Thomas' Church.

Another famous occupant of the same spot was the grocery business, John Williams and Sons. They were a successful chain of grocers who established businesses across

Manchester in the early 1900s. At their height they had over a dozen shops in the local area, and their director, Charles H. Scott, JP, lived in one of The Heatons' grandest house - West Bank in Heaton Mersey. The firm proclaimed to be experts in the supply of coffee and butter and their shops offered quality tea and coffee at 1 shilling per pound and 1/6d per pound respectively.

It's not only grocery provision which has a foothold in the history of Heaton Chapel. The present butcher's shop, Littlewoods, is continuing a tradition of meat provision in the area which goes back to the 19th century. There's actually been a butcher's shop there since 1860.

The opposite corner of the junction has always been dominated by the George and Dragon Hotel, a traditional, Victorian coaching inn. In 1824 the building located on this site was a farm which was eventually turned into a coaching inn. The pub originally advertised 'good stabling' reflecting the importance of its location on the

Above: **The George and Dragon, circa 1927**

Above right: **Manchester Road and School Lane junction, circa 1905**

Right: **Heaton Chapel village and Williams' Grocers, 1905**

main thoroughfare. It was first rebuilt in 1909, losing its distinctive balcony, and moving slightly further away from the road. More recently it used to have a full-size snooker table but this disappeared during recent modernisation. It originally served ale from Clarke's Reddish Brewery which, despite its name, operated from premises on Sandy Lane, Heaton Norris. It survived until 1963 when it was taken over by Boddingtons.

So, as the saying goes, you never know what's around the corner! Perhaps it's time to find out as you take a stroll around Heaton Chapel village. There's good food, fine beers and even a pavement café where you can sit and watch the world go by.

MATTERS OF LIFE AND DEATH

A Heatons Family Funeral Business

Funeral Directors George **Ball and Son, which sits at the corner of Portland Grove and Derby Range, has served families in The Heatons for five generations. It's part of the fabric of the area and it has a fascinating history.**

The building currently occupied by the business was at one time home to

the Heaton Moor Printing Company and was previously owned by Lookers Garage. Over the years George Ball & Son has been located in various properties around Portland Grove, Birch Avenue and Derby Range.

The earliest record of the business dates back to 1870 when it was opened by George Ball, the great grandfather of Margaret Arnison (nee Ball) who now runs the business with her son Daniel

and his wife Rachel. George Ball was the local master carpenter and coffin maker and it was from these skills that he became an undertaker of funerals.

The business was taken on by Margaret's grandfather, (also George Ball), who lived at number 10 Portland Grove. He was assisted by his sister, known by everyone locally (and even Margaret) simply as Nurse Ball, who was a nurse and midwife.

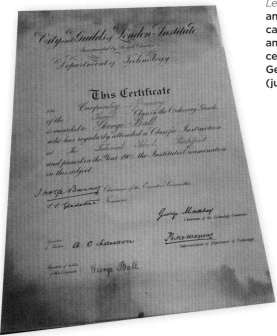

Left: **City and Guild's carpentry and joinery certificate for George (junior), 1903**

She lived at number 37 and used her skills to become the person in charge of laying out the deceased.

Margaret's grandmother, Elizabeth, took most of the responsibility for running things during WWI. George had been called up and was heavily involved in operations in the Somme. Thankfully he returned and the business continued successfully between the wars before it was taken over by Margaret's father, Sidney Ball. Sidney also did his service for 'King and Country', serving in the Royal Engineers, based on Salisbury Plain.

Grandfather George continued to contribute to the development of the company, notably opening Stockport's first chapel of rest, just behind the house at 37 Derby Range, in 1954. This was a very prestigious step, as prior to this the deceased would have been laid out and kept in their own home until suitable arrangements for the funeral could be made. Between the wars, George was also instrumental in introducing

motorised vehicles to the company. Previously, transportation of the coffin from the home of the deceased to the churchyard or crematorium would have been undertaken by horse and carriage.

Grandfather George was also a founder member of the Northern College of Embalming which he established along with other skilled individuals. George studied in Birmingham in the 1920s and was at the forefront of bringing such specialist skills into the funeral business.

Margaret finally took over the business in 1978. She had never thought of doing this, having been a teacher at Fylde Lodge High School before the birth of her two sons, but with guidance from her father embraced the role of funeral director. Today the business is as successful as it has ever been. A small office tucked away at the junction of two of The Heatons' most quaint roads providing a service quite out of proportion to its physical size.

Above: **Today George Ball's Funeral Service occupies the buildings which were once home to the Heaton Moor Printing Company**

Left: **Sidney Ball, at the steering wheel, with his employees on one of the first motorised vehicles owned by the company, circa 1930**

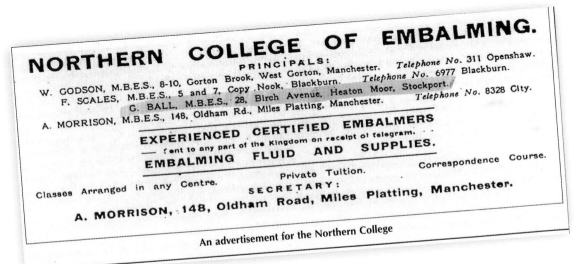

An advertisement for the Northern College

Above: **George Ball was a founder member of the Northern College of Embalming**

Pleasure Cruises and Commerce

Heaton Norris' Forgotten Canal

Left: **Wharf Street behind Albion Mill reminds us of the canal's existence**

Below: **The Navigaton pub gives a clue to the site of the canal terminus**

Left: **Aerial shot of the canal from 1927 with Albion Mill at the top of Lancashire Hill, in the bottom left hand corner. Today, Asda stands on the site of the factories**

We all have different ways of travelling in and out of The Heatons - walking and biking for those of us who are more health-conscious, but more often by bus, train and car. However, just over 200 years ago it was possible to cruise out of The Heatons on Stockport's very own canal!

The Industrial Revolution in Britain started from around 1760 and wealthy merchants and mill owners were looking for a cheap way to transport their goods safely and in large quantities. The Manchester to Ashton Canal was opened in 1796 and, just a year later, Stockport was linked into the canal system by a new spur which ran from between Locks 10 and 11 at Clayton, down into Heaton Norris at the top of Lancashire Hill.

The main purpose of the canal was the transportation of coal from the collieries around Ashton into Stockport. In addition, it was used to carry general cargo such as raw cotton to the local mills, returning with the manufactured goods. It also carried supplies of grain to William Nelstrop and Company's 'Albion Mill' in Heaton Norris. The canal was just over four miles long and was unusual

in that it didn't contain a single lock. It passed through Openshaw, Gorton, Debdale Park and Reddish before arriving at a wharf and warehouse complex at the top of Lancashire Hill. Today, the biggest reminders of its existence are the presence of the Navigation Pub just outside Albion Mill, and Wharf Street - which still runs behind the back of the premises.

There was however, an unexpected benefit for Heatons residents with the rise of a passenger boat service which sat side by side with the busy trade route. In May 1799, the Manchester Mercury gave notice that a passenger boat service would open between Heaton Norris and Piccadilly. The success of the service was immediate, the appeal to passengers being the relatively short journey time and the relative comfort of the boats compared to a rickety ride down cobbled streets into the city centre.

The initial operations saw boats leaving Heaton Norris for Manchester from 8am, the last boat returning from Piccadilly Wharf at 6pm. The service ran daily and its success was such that the service was expanded, with operators offering a two hour trip from Stockport to Stalybridge via the Ashton Canal and the newly

The Stockport Branch Canal

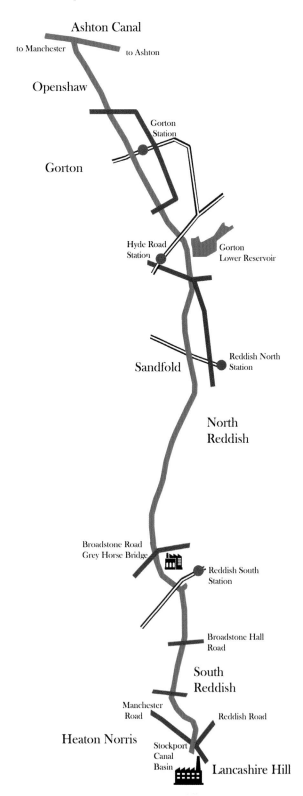

Ashton Canal

to Manchester   to Ashton

Openshaw

Gorton Station

Gorton

Hyde Road Station

Gorton Lower Reservoir

Reddish North Station

Sandfold

North Reddish

Broadstone Road Grey Horse Bridge

Reddish South Station

Broadstone Hall Road

South Reddish

Manchester Road

Reddish Road

Heaton Norris

Stockport Canal Basin

Lancashire Hill

opened Huddersfield Narrow Canal.

The fare from Heaton Norris into Manchester was one shilling for a front seat, and 8d (pennies) for a seat at the back (equivalent to around £4.00 and £2.65 in today's money). To travel into Stalybridge was slightly more expensive at 1s 3d for a seat in the front cabin and 9d for a seat at the back of the boat - passengers coming back the same day paid only half fare for the return leg of the journey. Such was the novelty of the new mode of transport that groups of people hired canal boats for the day and cruised between Heaton Norris, Manchester and Ashton at their leisure.

Sadly, the canal began to decline as a result of competition from the railways and roads. It started to fall into dereliction as early as 1922 and commercial traffic ceased altogether in the 1930s. The canal was dredged in the 1950s but this did not result in a resurrection of trade and it was finally abandoned in 1962. When the south mill of the two mills making up Broadstone Mill was demolished in 1965, the thousands of bricks were used to fill that part of the abandoned canal. The line of the canal can still be followed though as it has been turned into a surfaced pathway along most of its length.

So, next time you're packed into a bus, standing shoulder to shoulder with commuters on an early morning train, or crawling at snail's pace in your car up the A6, think back enviously to those days when travellers could enjoy a leisurely journey into the very heart of the city, arriving fresh and unflurried from their very own Heatons cruise!

Right: **The old route of the Stockport Branch Canal**

Far right: **Broadstone Hall Bridge, 2018. The cottages have gone and a new bridge has replaced the old one**

The canal at Grey Horse Bridge spanning the top of Broadstone Road, circa 1905 Broadstone Mill in the background is under construction

Proud to be part of local life

The Moor Top 1960s

The Moor Top today

Investing in the future of the The Heatons

THE
MOOR TOP

PUB & KITCHEN

VINO · CERVEZA · GINEBRA

LA CANTINA

BAR · TAPAS

Burgons Tea
Emporium, 1904

HIGH TEA, HATS AND HABERDASHERY

112 Heaton Moor Road

Most definitely 112 Heaton Moor Road is a corner plot with history, and one which, over the past 125 years, has served Heaton Moor well. It's been a bit of a chameleon, changing its colours to suit a number of commercial purposes

- in its day it has been home to banks, lavish tearooms, high-class drapers and firms of solicitors.

The earliest photograph of the front of the building is from the turn of the 20th century when it was occupied by Burgon's, the tea merchants which had branches across the North West,

including shops in Salford, Oldham and Bolton. Within the shop, the Tea Department proclaimed to offer 'a greater variety than that of any other house' and sold what they termed '3 Capital Ts': the Kintuck Blend, the Burgon Blend and the Special Blend - all of which were available for customers to sample in the café. The

Above: **Cliff and Brown Milliners, 1917**

Below: **The carving commissioned by Martins is still visible on the side of the building today**

Coffee Department roasted coffee on the premises and boasted that it was produced using the most up-to-date machinery and that every market had been searched for the best quality coffee.

Photographs from 1918 show the premises occupied by Cliff and Brown, drapers and milliners. The premises extended into Shaw Road and displayed a sign proclaiming themselves: 'The Noted House for Millinery, Fancy Drapery, Blouses and Underclothing.' The front windows of the shop sported a fine selection of hats, reflecting the importance of fashionable headgear to the well-dressed Victorian. A good hat was the sign of a gentleman, and men returning from fighting in the war were obliged to wear a hat for a certain length of time as part of their demobilisation process.

Between 1888 and the early 1920s, the side of the premises had been occupied by The Lancashire and Yorkshire Bank, with an entrance directly off Heaton Moor Road. In 1928 the bank amalgamated with Martins

Bank. The front of the building was re-designed, spacious windows added to both the front and side elevations, and a stylish entrance was added, with the word 'Bank' engraved in stone across the top of the door.

However, by June 1936 the premises were showing signs of decay and it was decided that the building should be demolished and a new one erected with a design more in keeping with the bank's commercial connections in the district. In January 1937, plans by Manchester architect Joseph Holt, were approved by the bank's committee and in March they accepted the tender of Hibbert and Penn Ltd, (contactors) of Edgeley to demolish the old building and construct a new one for £5,390 (around £225,000 in today's money). The new branch opened on 2nd May 1938 and was described in the bank's promotional literature as being 'in Georgian style, with a façade of warm-coloured, sand-faced bricks with Derbyshire stone dressing.'

FOUR DEPARTMENTS OF

BURGONS

WELL-KNOWN AND OLD-ESTABLISHED BUSINESS.

The Tea Department

offers a greater variety than that of any other house, the different requirements of certain palates are sure to be met with in one or other of their blends. They call attention to the following well-known Teas :—

3 CAPITAL T'S

The **KINTUCK** Blend - 1/6
The **BURGON** Blend - 2/-
The **SPECIAL** Blend - 2/8
(As used at the Cafe).

The Coffee Department

is kept to the highest standard. They roast on the premises with the most up-to-date machinery. They search every market for the best quality, and sell at the lowest prices.

Provision and Butter Department

is one that requires great attention. It is supervised with the greatest care, so that every article shall be as described, and such as the customers may rely upon.

Italian and Proprietory Goods Dept.

Burgons keep in stock perhaps the largest assortment of any house in the Kingdom The great majority of the articles are sold much under the fixed prices.

112 HEATON MOOR ROAD, STOCKPORT

Left: **Burgons advert, 1904**

An interesting feature of the building, (which can still be seen today), is the stone carving high above the windows on the Heaton Moor Road side. The carving was commissioned by Martins Bank at a cost of £107 (around £4,500 in today's money) and contains a grasshopper (the original sign of London branches of Martins), the Liver Bird, (reflecting the history of the bank in Liverpool), and two sheaves of corn - which could be a reflection on the semi-

rural nature of The Heatons in the 1930s.

Martins Bank eventually closed and the building was taken over by Barclays Bank on 15th December 1969. Barclays remained until the early 1990s, since when the building has had a bit of a chequered history, having been home to a wholesale fabric business, a firm of solicitors and a bridal emporium. Inside, the original interior features, such as the large cellars with vaults, and the beamed, lofty, open-plan hall

with mezzanine level, have largely been preserved. Currently owned by the Northern Restaurants group, one of The Heatons' landmark buildings waits patiently for the next phase of its history.

As a company, Northern Restaurants is also looking to the past for a model of good business practice. We all nip into one of our local Co-op stores - they're an established part of shopping in The Heatons. But how many of us think of the history and philosophy of

Above:
Lancashire and Yorkshire Bank, 1905

Left: **Martins Bank, 1938**

the movement which took hold a few miles north in Rochdale in the mid-19th century? The principles are sound and were constructed and refined by Robert Owen, very much a believer in the self-help work ethic. He believed improving everyone's personal environment would lead to improved circumstances for all, which in turn would lead to goodness.

Now, Northern Restaurants group is planning a modern-day cooperative initiative. Starting with Northern Restaurants' businesses in The Heatons and Stockport, there'll be a part management buy-out and profit share enterprise for the current team. A percentage of the money generated from the new cooperative model will also be allocated to local good causes in the same way today's Co-op operates. The introduction of a cooperative style profit share scheme will bring stability to the company's restaurants and bars across The Heatons and allow for something to be put back into the community. It shows that it's not just our historical buildings we should be reviving in the 21st century, but some business practices too.

A Breath of Fresh Air

Living in Norris Bank

You probably don't give it a second glance, as you hasten down Didsbury Road after passing through the lights at Bank Hall Road. Destined for the motorway, you'll hardly notice the church and the lines of red brick houses bearing names from a bygone era: Endymion, The Elms, Fleensop.

Yet the area of Norris Bank and the start of Didsbury Road would have been an important route in and out of Stockport as early as the 1900s. The road surface would have been cobbled and rough and traffic would have been heavy, with horses straining to pull fully laden carts up the long rise past Norris Bank House and Bank Cottage to Bank Hall at the top of the hill - and on to Heaton

Mersey and Didsbury. The houses in Norris Bank become grander as the road climbed, because those with money would have wanted to live with the fine views across the town to the hills and fresh air blown in from the Peak District.

The area around Brighton Road, just past the now-demolished Club House pub, would have been much less wealthy than the area further up

The area around Brighton Road was a quiet, semi-rural spot

Norris Bank

the rise. There were still a number of factories nearby which demanded that their employees worked long and tiring shifts, in rooms with noisy machinery and no health and safety regulations in place to protect them.

But for most of the workers, heading home each evening, it was the first breath of fresh air as they trudged wearily up the slope of Travis Brow, away from the noise and pollution of the factories and railway yards, possibly calling in at the Club House for a well-earned drink before heading home. On reaching the corner shop at Norris Avenue there would have been a feeling that the industrial world was left behind and that they'd entered an altogether more rural environment. The photograph shows that the shop was doing a good trade in seeds, (which are advertised on the signs on the front door), giving an indication of the semi-agricultural nature of the area.

Corner shops were very important to the local community, selling a variety of goods such as foodstuffs

and hardware as well as a range of agricultural supplies. The shop would also have been suitably valued by the children in the picture as it undoubtedly had a good range of sweets and other 'goodies': bullseyes, pear drops, liquorice sticks and humbugs would have been amongst their particular favourites.

A little further along, St Martin's Church, a relative newcomer to worship in The Heatons, was commissioned in 1901 by the then Bishop of Manchester, James Moorhouse. It added to the sense of community in Norris Bank, giving status to the area and alleviating the need for local worshippers to take a long walk to St John's in Heaton Mersey or St Paul's up on the Moor.

Just past St Martin's, the land to the right of the road, (which is now part of the recreational open space allocated after the building of the Wittenbury Road housing estate), was a pretty area called Meadowbank. It bordered Norris Hill Farm and swept around the top of Crescent Park. It was partly swallowed up by the building of new

Above: **The terraced houses lost much of their front garden space with the widening of Didsbury Road**

Right: **Construction of the first houses on Meadowbank in the 1930s**

houses in the 1930s, but the remaining sweep of greenery still reminds us of the once pastoral nature of the area.

Today there's a mix of the old and new, with flats and houses from the modern era and a bit less green space for homeowners since the widening of Didsbury Road in the 70s. The Victorians built their houses and terraces with long front gardens but sadly they were cut back to accommodate the ever-increasing traffic of the 20th century which now dominates the old trade route. However, the green pockets of Norris Bank which remain serve as a reminder of the importance of preserving our treasured open spaces.

Above: **The corner shop at Norris Avenue provided the community with a good range of supplies, 1904**

Left: **The sweep down Norris Bank afforded wealthier residents fine views across the town, 1920s**

A FORGOTTEN VICTORIAN CORNER

Moor Top Place

The area around Moor Top has always been a traditional shopping area for Heatons residents. The names of the businesses may have changed but the range of goods and services offered has remained fairly constant. The familiar row of shops on the eastern side of Heaton Moor Road (think Bramley Carpets and Sue Ryder) was built in 1872, and by 1915 the row had been extended south into Moorside Road. The area takes its name from the position on which it stands, which once marked the southern end of the Moor as it bordered Clifton Road. Moor Top holds an elevated position, being one of the highest points in The Heatons at 225ft above sea level. Before the building of the houses and shops, it would have offered spectacular views towards Stockport and south towards Alderley Edge.

The small thoroughfare of Moor Top Place sits almost unnoticed as you pass through the centre of the village, but this corner is a hidden gem of history which has undergone some changes but still retains much of the character of its past. The most significant change to the area came in the 1970s with the demolition of a row of Victorian houses on the north side of Moor Top Place (the side nearest The Savoy), and the removal of four even larger properties on the southern side of Hawthorn Grove (the side furthest away from The Savoy). All these properties had substantial gardens, and the demolition left a large plot of land ripe for development. The developers moved in with the result that we now have a row of white modern buildings, shops below with flats above, where once stood Victorian splendour.

The premises on the corner of Moor Top Place and Heaton Moor Road is

A view of Moor Top Place, 1905

Boys gather outside Moor Top shops. Note that the post box is actually on the road, 1905

Wensveen's Grocery Store and Dewhurst's Butcher's Shop, 1970s

currently occupied by Nettl, a website development and printing business, run by Rajeev Arora. There's a strong Arora family connection with the building on the corner - it has not always been about displays and desktops. From 1988 the business was run by Rajeev's mother and father. It was a popular clothes shop called Patches, distinguishable by the bright, multi-coloured awning which was a feature of the front of the shop. Rajeev remembers that the business spread across two shops previously owned by Wensveen's grocery and store and Dewhurt's butcher's shop. Patches was very popular with locals and is remembered fondly for what Rajeev's mother termed the 'Cuddly Sizes Corner' where those requiring larger than average items of attire could browse the clothes. Rajeev's father also recalls discovering a huge, stone, meat-freezing room in a corridor connecting the two shops, which had laid untouched for some years after he took over the shop. Patches closed in 2003 and was taken over by Main and

Main Estate agents, until 2008 when Rajeev opened it as a printing business.

Behind the shops, the area retains plenty of connections with its past. Some of the old Victorian and Edwardian terraces are still there tucked away in a shady spot surrounded by mature trees. There's the local garage (Roadside Garage), still doing plenty of business, much like the one that was there in the early 1900s. Back then the site was owned by Thomas O'Donnell, a coach proprietor, who specialised in the provision of landaus, broughams, and wagonettes. You'd have also found there local handyman Ernest Downes, whose skills were in building and joinery.

So next time you're drifting along Heaton Moor Road, take the time to turn off, nip along Moor Top Place between Nettl and the modern row of shops, and stroll along the path round to Hawthorn Grove. It's a part of The Heatons that time seems to have forgotten, with only the rear view of the modern development reminding us of the bustle of 21st century life along Heaton Moor Road just a stone's throw away.

Above right: **Local tradesmen's sign on Moor Top Place, 1902**

Right: **The junction of Hawthorn Terrace and Moor Top Place, 1970s**

Left: **Rajeev Arora and his mother outside Patches, circa 1990**

River View Cottages, 1920

The Fifth Heaton

Reddish and its Vale

They say that George Martin was the fifth Beatle and that without him the greatest group in the history of pop music would not have reached such dizzy heights of stardom in the 1960s. But what about our own 'Fab Four' of Mersey, Moor, Norris and Chapel and our own fifth Heaton? It's there in the background and, like George Martin, it's a bit different from the other four.

Ecclesiastically, Reddish even shares its name with its four near neighbours. Parish registers for St Mary's Church record that in 1864, Reddish was a township and chapelry in Manchester which was known as Heaton-Reddish. Even today, the official name given to this fine old parish church sitting on Reddish Road is St Mary Heaton, Heaton Reddish.

So, what would our fifth Heaton bring to the Fab Four? Undoubtedly its picturesque Vale, which sits in land which falls away from the neat clusters of redbrick housing to the east of Reddish Road, far outstrips any open green space to be found within The Four Heatons.

Reddish Vale offers a pleasant escape from the busy suburban environment which surrounds it and its long history supports tales of farming, milling, textile manufacturing and quarrying. Take

a walk into its green and pleasant surroundings and you enter a world which has been shaped over centuries and contains reminders of the part it has played in the lives of ordinary people. Sadly, some of the buildings, such as River View Cottages, are no longer there. Condemned as unfit for habitation in 1961, their last inhabitants were two sisters, Mrs Emma Adshead and Mrs Nelly Ridgway, (both in their eighties), who were reluctant to move from the peace and tranquillity of River View. They had lived there all their lives, their father having been employed at the Calico Print Works which once stood in the Vale. Similarly, the nine houses which stood under the railway viaduct were pulled down in 1914 despite offering a service to local walkers who were sold refreshments by their enterprising inhabitants.

Dominating the landscape today is the imposing 17 arched viaduct, built by the Sheffield and Midland Railways Committee in order to complete their Romiley to Ashbury line. The viaduct drastically changed the outlook of the valley and it is said that a local witch, who was unhappy with it being built, put a curse on anyone who dared count the arches!

Reddish Vale Farm has been associated with the area since the 19th Century, offering a riding school, small animal farm and café.

Nestling against the banks of the River Tame is Reddish Vale Golf Club. Over a hundred years ago, Frank William Reed was hitting golf balls on a piece of land, known as Wilcock Eye. So taken was he with the surroundings he purchased an imposing manor house, South Cliffe, leased a hundred acres of land, and commissioned Dr Alistair McKenzie to inspect the area

and design the course. McKenzie went on to become one of the era's foremost golf course designers, constructing courses across the world including the Augusta National, home of the US Open. Today the course must rank as one of the most picturesque in the country, as its fairways twist and turn around the Tame and in many quarters is considered to be one of

the top 100 courses in the world.

So next time you fancy a day out, but you don't want to pack the kids in the car and drive for miles, pay Reddish and its Vale a visit. You'll find all sorts happening there, from family fun days and nature walks, through to organised archaeological digs. You could even play some Beatles tracks in the car on the way.

Above: **The sweep of Reddish Vale today**

Below: **The Royal Train passes over the viaduct and cottages, June 12th 1905**

THE CIRCULATION OF KNOWLEDGE

The Lending Library Boom

Far left **The sign for the lending library is displayed but it has already moved further down Heaton Moor Road, 1908**

Left **Heaton Moor Library in the 1950s**

There's no doubt that reading has always been a popular pastime in The Heatons. The main library in Heaton Moor was established in 1950, sited in the home of the Barlow family on Thornfield Road. It moved to its present premises, just around the corner, in 1992 and has been an important focal point for the community ever since. The Children's Society

book shop, situated close by, is always packed with readers young and old, sifting through its wide selection of second-hand books.

Prior to the opening of the public library, The Heatons had its own circulating library, which occupied at least two different premises along Heaton Moor Road. Its first known location was near the junction of Heaton Moor Road and Shaw Road, but at the time of the

picture, (taken in 1908), it had already moved further north to occupy the building next to Blaggs Hardware - with only its sign remaining above the fancy goods shop. By the 1930s the circulating library had become well-established, and was a focal point for avid readers in The Heatons. So, what exactly were circulating libraries?

Well, they were similar to the public libraries which we have today, but in fact they were private businesses.

TERMS OF SUBSCRIPTION.

Commencing at any date.

SINGLE AND FAMILY SUBSCRIPTION.

	Six Months. £ s. d.	Twelve Months. £ s. d.
ONE VOLUME AT ONE TIME	0 12 0 ...	1 1 0
FOUR DITTO DITTO	1 2 0 ...	2 2 0
EIGHT DITTO DITTO	1 14 0 ...	3 3 0

Subscribers are entitled to exchange their Books at pleasure—not oftener than once a-day.

The leading Periodicals may be obtained, one at a time, on the day of publication,—each being counted as one volume.

Above: **Heaton Moor Lending Library, 1936**

Left: **Lending Library subscription rates, 1936**

Free public libraries did not exist in the early part of the 20th century, so patrons of the circulating libraries were charged a fee for borrowing the books and penalised if the items were lost, damaged or not returned by the due date. To supplement the profits, and offset the cost of buying new stock, the libraries often sold stationery and newspapers as well as occasionally dealing in the sale of hats, medicines, teas, perfumes, and tobacco - even providing barbering services!

The circulating library would have been important to The Heatons, which in the early part of the century, was well populated with wealthy families. These members of the middle and upper classes benefited from education, money and leisure time - which meant they were able to indulge in reading and so would have been primary users of the library. Subscriptions were based on the number of books to be borrowed at a time - so in a large family, where

both children and parents wished to borrow books regularly, the costs increased substantially. Whilst a yearly subscription to the circulating library was cheap compared to the cost of purchasing books, it was still probably beyond what a typical working-class individual could afford, particularly as fines for damage or misuse usually equated to the full replacement cost of the book. Despite these costs, circulating libraries were extremely popular in the first part of the 20th century. They allowed access to more books than even the middle classes could reasonably afford, and they were also a popular social destination where people could meet and discuss their reading - much like the reading groups which exist in The Heatons today.

Nevertheless, they were occasionally viewed with concern and, just as we worry about the social implications of TV and the internet today, there were fears about the kinds of books women, children, and teens could access. Also,

there were schools of thought which objected to reading as a form of dignified idleness and, particularly in Victorian times, there were concerns about the dangers of the content of some novels, and how they might corrupt the minds of women. Despite these concerns, the reading of novels and the use of the circulating libraries only increased in popularity.

Most circulating libraries survived well into the 20th century, before two things contributed to their downfall. The rise of public libraries and free borrowing created access to literature for all classes, and the reduced cost of printing made buying books an attractive option for many people. However, one thing is certain - the love for books and reading has not diminished in The Heatons. Just pop into the Children's Society book shop, or The Heatons Library, and share your thirst for knowledge and adventure with your fellow Heatons bibliophiles.

A Reminder of Medieval Traditions

Almshouses for the Elderly and Needy

At first glance, they are completely out of character with the surrounding architecture. A cluster of buildings of seemingly Gothic extravagance, which, on a dark and rainy night, might make even the bravest soul hesitate before stepping through the imposing stone gateway, the shadows from the trees flickering across the narrow pathway.

James Ainsworth of Heaton Norris left provision in his will for these twelve, semi-detached cottages, with gardens and stone entrance archways, to be built on Green Lane in 1907. James was a wealthy local businessman who wished to provide accommodation for some of the neediest and most deserving residents of The Heatons. The bequest in his will stated that they were to be allocated to old people

"whose honourable record and needy circumstances make such shelter and assistance in their declining years well-deserved.'" Each property was designed to have its own garden at the rear, so that residents could focus industriously on growing vegetables as part of a regime to keep them active! The Grade II listed buildings were built by Pierce and Son in 1907, and the red and grey brick design, with red

Left: **The picturesque Prescott Almshouses sit at the side of Reddish Road**

Below left: **The almshouses on Green Lane today**

Right: **Prescott's bust above the door of no 399**

terracotta dressings, is very distinctive. There are twelve properties, with both end houses having corner turrets with lead domes. Their design is ingenious and compact. Each cottage has a small entrance hall, a scullery, a parlour, a kitchen, a privy (toilet) and coal storage. The first residents moved in around 1907 and the homes have continued to be allocated to retired people ever since.

Reddish also has its own row of quaint Victorian almshouses - on the corner of Reddish Road and Greg Street. They actually pre-date those on Green Lane, being established in 1878 when Stockport drysalter W.W. Prescott died, bequeathing £5,000 to the aged and poor. Like those in The Heatons they have a garden, but this time at the front, with a paved yard at the rear. Around £2,000 was spent on building the row of almshouses, and the only rules left by the benefactor

were that tenants must be aged 60 or over, come from 'the ancient townships of Reddish, Bredbury and Denton' and be a Protestant. Today the whole row is a Grade II listed building and bears the name of their benefactor and his stone bust above the door of number 399.

Almshouses, of course, are not a new concept. They've been part of the social landscape for some considerable time. In Britain, they date from around the 10th century and stemmed from the Christian movement to provide a place of residence for poor, old and distressed people. They were originally often referred to as bede-houses and the residents as bedesmen or bedeswomen. The old English definition of a bedesman is a 'man of prayer' and occupants of almshouses were often expected to pray for their benefactor in return for his hospitality. In the Middle Ages, the majority of

hospitals functioned as almshouses, with many long-term inmates supported by charitable donations from various sources. The oldest still in existence is the Hospital of St. Cross in Winchester, dating from about 1132.

Many of the early almshouses in England were set up with the purpose of benefiting the soul of their founder and raising his standing in the eyes of God. As a result, they often incorporated a chapel to make it easy for the residents to offer up their prayers.

The almshouses on Green Lane have changed little since their initial construction, although the whole terrace underwent a period of modernisation in 1991. Today, they are let by the Arcon Housing Association to the over-60s residents of Heaton Norris. Like their counterparts in Reddish the row of buildings is Grade II listed.

ABOUT THE AUTHOR

Phil Page is a writer and photographer who has lived in The Heatons since 1981. He is a former secondary school English teacher and associate tutor in teacher training at Manchester Metropolitan University. He has published several local history books for Amberley Publishers with his co-writer, Ian Littlechilds, and has been MOOR's history features writer since 2014.

About MOOR Magazine

MOOR - The magazine for The Four Heatons, was established in 2010. The magazine is delivered free of charge to 10,500 homes and businesses every two months.